GETTING A PhD IN LAW

Getting a PhD in Law is a unique guide to obtaining the degree of Doctor of Philosophy of Law in the UK. While there is a wide range of study guides for PhD students in the social sciences and other science-based disciplines, there is very little information available on the process of obtaining a PhD in law. Research degrees in law share some attributes with those in related disciplines such as the humanities and social sciences. However, legal methodology and the place of the PhD in law in the young lawyer's career create unique challenges that have not been addressed by existing guides. *Getting a PhD in Law* fills this clear gap in the market, providing an accessible guide to the PhD process from topic selection to thesis publication. This readable and informative guide draws on interviews and case studies with PhD students, supervisors and examiners. *Getting a PhD in Law* will be essential reading for the growing numbers of PhD students in the UK's many law schools—and those internationally who wish to learn from UK best practice.

GW00643714

Getting a PhD in Law

Caroline Morris
and
Cian Murphy

·HART·
PUBLISHING

OXFORD AND PORTLAND, OREGON
2011

Hart Publishing

An imprint of Bloomsbury Publishing Plc

Hart Publishing Ltd
Kemp House
Chawley Park
Cumnor Hill
Oxford OX2 9PH
UK

Bloomsbury Publishing Plc
50 Bedford Square
London
WC1B 3DP
UK

www.hartpub.co.uk
www.bloomsbury.com

Published in North America (US and Canada) by
Hart Publishing
c/o International Specialized Book Services
920 NE 58th Avenue, Suite 300
Portland, OR 97213-3786
USA

www.isbs.com

**HART PUBLISHING, the Hart/Stag logo, BLOOMSBURY and the
Diana logo are trademarks of Bloomsbury Publishing Plc**

British Library Cataloguing-in-Publication Data
A catalogue record for this book is available from the British Library.

ISBN: 978-1-84113-306-5

Typeset by Compuscript Ltd, Shannon

To find out more about our authors and books visit www.hartpublishing.co.uk. Here you will
find extracts, author information, details of forthcoming events and the option to sign up for our
newsletters.

Acknowledgements

Writing a book is very much a collaborative endeavour. This book would probably not have been written and is very much improved thanks to the input of the following people. For their time, and their willingness to share their ideas and their experiences we are very grateful. Of course any errors are ours and ours alone.

The following friends and colleagues read some of the book in draft form and offered useful advice and suggestions: Diego Acosta, Mark Bennett, Penny Green, Piet Eeckhout, Bevan Marten, Noel McGrath, Harry Nikolaidis, Federico Ortino, Eloise Scotford and Rachael Walsh. We also benefited from the questions and suggestions of the participants of the 'Getting a PhD in Law' seminar at King's College London in the summer of 2010. Thanks are also due to Elimma Ezeani, Becca Franssen, Marta Iljadica and Anastasia Lee who allowed us to include their thesis titles in chapter two.

We owe particular thanks to those who took the time to contact us through our website and offer us their thoughts on their PhD experience. They cannot, due to space restrictions and the desire for anonymity, be listed here—but you know who you are and we are grateful for your candour.

Richard Hart and his colleagues at Hart Publishing supported this project from the outset and have proven time and again to be wonderful people to work with. We very much appreciate the support Hart Publishing has shown this and our other book projects in recent years.

The last and most heartfelt thanks must go to Richard and Sarah, for their support while we were completing our own theses and their tolerance as we revisited the experience while writing this volume. This book is dedicated to their patience.

Table of Contents

Acknowledgements... v
Table of Contents.. vii
Introduction: About this Book ix

1. Why Do a PhD in Law?.. 1
  The PhD and Other Degrees 2
  The Value of a PhD in Law 4
  The PhD and Your Career 6
  To PhD or not to PhD?.. 10

2. Preparing for the PhD.. 11
  The 'Thesis' 11
  Choosing a PhD Topic.. 13
  Types of PhD Programme... 16
  Choosing an Institution and Supervisor.. 19
  Making Your Application 23
  The F-word (Funding) 26
  Conclusion 27

3. Legal Research Methodologies 28
  The Importance of Methodology.. 29
  Types of Legal Research Methodologies....................................... 30
  Choosing the Most Appropriate Methodology 38
  Developing the Research Project 39
  Conclusion 40

4. Researching an Original Thesis 41
  The Research and Writing Process 41
  Developing an Original Thesis 43
  Ethical Issues in Legal Research 48
  Research Aids.. 52
  Conclusion 57

5. Supervision 58
  The Supervisory Relationship.. 58
  Making the Best of Your Supervisor... 66

Supervision Problems 68
Conclusion 72

6. PhD Problems 73
Someone Else Wrote My PhD! 73
Boredom and Lack of Motivation 75
Financial Problems 77
Writer's Block 78
Health Problems 79
Conclusion: Getting Help and Solving Problems 81

7. Writing-up 83
Knowing When to Write-up 83
Turning a Collection of Chapters into a Thesis 85
Good Legal Writing 86
Producing the Final Draft 90
Conclusion 91

8. Examining the PhD 93
The Viva 94
The Examiners 94
Preparing for the Viva 97
In the Examination 98
After the Viva 103
Conclusion 105

9. Publishing Your Work 106
Why You Need to Publish 106
What to Publish During Your PhD 107
Where to Publish Your Work 109
Publishing From Your Thesis 114
Conclusion 119

10. Building A Career 120
Teaching and Research 120
The Need to Network 124
Presenting Your Work at a Conference 128
Conclusion 132

Appendix A: Useful Resources 133
Appendix B: Funding Organisations in the UK 137
Appendix C: Blawgs 139

Short Bibliography 141
Index 143

Introduction: About this Book

This book seeks to provide a readable and informative guide to the research degree process. The doctoral degree can still be treated as something of an oddity among lawyers. If you're *that* clever, doctoral researchers are often asked, why aren't you in practice? Nonetheless modern law schools are more and more coming around to the idea of their doctoral cohorts as key parts of the life of the school and you should find that the degree is better understood now that it was a decade ago. Other academic disciplines—in particular the social sciences—are well-served with how-to guides. During our own degrees we drew on the wisdom of Phillips and Pugh's *How to get a PhD: A Handbook for Students and Their Supervisors*—a book which has gone through four editions since its first publication in 1987. Dunleavy's *Authoring a PhD: How to Plan, Draft, Write & Finish a Doctoral Thesis or Dissertation* provides further sage advice—especially for the more humanities-oriented parts of our theses. However, during our studies we felt keenly the absence of a book aimed at us as academic lawyers. Though we could learn from guides for social scientists and humanities researchers, they did not capture the unique nature of the law doctorate. Law cannot be pigeon-holed as a social science or arts and humanities discipline—while it borrows from both it cannot be considered a sub-discipline of either. It was our own difficulty in obtaining good advice on the process of getting a PhD in law which more than anything else sparked this book into life.

A PhD in law is, naturally, unique. We have written this book to address that experience undertaken by hundreds of doctoral candidates across the world every year. While the experiences we have drawn on are largely from those in universities in Britain and Ireland we believe there are lessons here for doctoral researchers throughout the common law world and even farther afield. We use a wide range of anecdotes throughout this book to illustrate the points we make. These have been gleaned from our own experiences and those of colleagues, from the many doctoral students we've met at conferences and seminars and through various online and offline communities. We've changed facts here and there to protect identities and in places we've combined two tales into one. But at the heart of each anecdote is the story of someone else's problem or solution—we hope you find inspiration or at least comfort in dealing with your own. If you have a story that we haven't told then be sure to get in touch! We continue to be interested in the whole doctoral research experience and it is through sharing experiences that the whole process can be demystified for those still undergoing it. The anecdotes are marked out by italicised text throughout the book and are intended to help you appreciate that you are not the first person to experience the challenges of the doctoral research process.

We have covered the PhD experience from the initial idea of undertaking the degree right through to publication and early career building. As a result, while we hope the book makes an interesting cover-to-cover read, it is likely that some chapters will become more relevant than others at different stages of the research degree process. The first, second and tenth chapters provide some useful background information and guidance on the PhD process and early career issues that will be helpful throughout your degree. At the outset of your research project you may find it useful to read these chapters in detail and skim through the book to get an idea of what advice can be found in which chapters. Then, as you approach different points in your progress, you can re-read those chapters as appropriate. Chapters three to seven deal with the heart of the law PhD experience from design through to research and writing and the problems you might encounter along the way. Chapter eight addresses the PhD viva; chapter nine the questions about what and where to publish during and after the PhD. In the appendices we have gathered together some resources and information about funding bodies which we hope you will find useful.

We wish you the very best as you embark on your research degree. It is an incomparable experience but one which, if successful, will be amongst the most rewarding in your life. We hope this book helps a little with the ups and downs that lie ahead. Good luck!

Caroline Morris

Cian Murphy

8 February 2011

1

Why Do a PhD in Law?

An article in the 18 December 2010 issue of *The Economist* was entitled 'The disposable academic' and argued that the system for research degrees was exploitative of some of the most talented young minds of a generation. It opened by observing:

> In most countries a PhD is a basic requirement for a career in academia. It is an introduction to the world of independent research—a kind of intellectual masterpiece, created by an apprentice in close collaboration with a supervisor. The requirements to complete one vary enormously between countries, universities and even subjects. Some students will first have to spend two years working on a master's degree or diploma. Some will receive a stipend; others will pay their own way. Some PhDs involve only research, some require classes and examinations and some require the student to teach undergraduates. A thesis can be dozens of pages in mathematics, or many hundreds in history. As a result, newly minted PhDs can be as young as their early 20s or world-weary forty-somethings.

Despite the disheartening tone of the article, this opening salvo certainly captures the disparate nature of the PhD community. There may be a typical PhD student but if there is we certainly haven't met him or her. Even within law schools there is a great variety of nationalities, ages, professional backgrounds and, of course, research interests. But how do you end up as a doctoral student?

Deciding what to do when you graduate can be one of the most difficult choices you face in the later years of your degree. For many, the choice is simple. The budding lawyer will complete a professional training course and seek a pupillage at chambers or a training contract with a firm. Others will take different routes, as a degree in law can be a useful foundation for a career in journalism, business or politics. However, not all students seek employment in the legal or other professions. Some remain in university and further their studies. Others who do begin their careers in practice later decide they would like to pursue an academic career and so return to university. For a few brave souls, the university experience will lead to doctoral studies—three or four years of independent research leading to the award of the university's highest degree.

This chapter addresses several preliminary issues that you should think about before seriously considering a PhD in law. It sets out the options for further study in law after graduation and explores the answers to several common questions about the PhD in law. These questions include:

— What is a PhD and how does it relate to other postgraduate degrees?
— What is the intrinsic value of completing a PhD?
— How will having a PhD help your career?

Once you have answered these questions you will be in a better position to decide whether or not the PhD in law is the degree for you.

THE PhD AND OTHER DEGREES

A PhD is a type of university degree. The abbreviation, PhD (sometimes DPhil), is derived from the Latin phrase *philosophiae doctor* which means Doctor of Philosophy. The term 'PhD' may also be used to describe the doctoral thesis—a body of work produced in the course of the degree—which we will explore in further detail in chapter two. The PhD as we know it was first awarded in 1828 by the Friedrich Wilhelm University, an institution that is now known as the Humboldt University in Berlin. From there, the degree spread across the world. In time the doctoral degree arrived in the UK where today there are thousands of researchers undertaking doctoral studies across the country. Despite having 'philosophy' in the title, a PhD can be obtained in most, if not all, academic disciplines, with the Doctor of Philosophy in Law the subject of our book. The PhD has traditionally been considered a form of apprenticeship for life in the academy. However, in recent years universities and governments have begun to acknowledge that not all who complete a research degree will want—or be able—to obtain a post in a university. As a result there is increasing emphasis on transferable skills and the ability to work across disciplines. While these developments may improve the overall training provided by research degrees, they put greater pressure on doctoral candidates who must not only produce a defensible thesis, but also engage in an often-intensive training programme. A PhD today looks different from one completed a decade ago—and it may look very different again in 10 or 20 years' time.

Deciding whether or not to pursue a doctorate requires an examination of the research degree alongside other options. The PhD is only one of several types of postgraduate degrees available in law. Many, if not most PhD students will already have completed a Masters degree in law or a related subject before embarking on a doctorate. Consider the admissions criteria for three UK law schools' PhD programmes:

> The candidate should have achieved, or be expected to achieve, at least a strong Merit in a Master's degree in law or a related discipline, with strong evidence of

research and writing ability. This will normally involve achieving a strong Merit in a dissertation component of the Master's degree. Candidates who do not meet these criteria will only be admitted if the prospective supervisor makes a case for admission based on the candidate's broader work experience. (King's College London)

Our minimum standard for admission is a good Upper Second Class honours or equivalent. For those applying to read for an MPhil or PhD, we have a strong preference for a recognised Master's degree for which we normally expect an average grade of at least 65% (or equivalent). Those without a Master's degree are expected to provide alternative evidence of ability to successfully undertake high quality written research. (University of Durham)

A minimum classification of 2.1 in their first degree (or equivalent) and, preferably, a Masters degree (or Masters degree pending). (University of Westminster)

It's clear from these excerpts that many universities will require you to have not just a good undergraduate degree but also a relevant Masters degree. The Master of Laws degree typically takes the form of an LLM (from the Latin, *Legum Magister*), although one may alternatively receive an MA, MSc, MRes, MLitt, MPhil, MJur or BCL. Whatever the degree title, Masters degrees usually fit one of two models: taught Masters degrees and Masters degrees by research. A taught Masters degree usually involves the student completing several modules of advanced legal study in addition to a research dissertation. On the other hand a Masters degree by research involves a large research project and fewer, if any, taught courses. Whether you choose to undertake a taught or research Masters degree before your PhD will depend in part on what you are trying to achieve. If you wish to further your knowledge in a broad, but still somewhat specialised area of law while keeping the option of further study available then a taught degree may be right for you. If you are more confident about your existing knowledge and would like to see if you enjoy research then an MRes or LLM by research may be more appropriate. We discuss how you can prepare for your PhD in detail in chapter two. However, even before you consider writing a research proposal and contacting potential supervisors, it is possible to prepare yourself for a doctorate.

So, how should you go about setting yourself up to complete a doctorate? If you are a final year undergraduate student and you wish to pursue a doctorate, you should seriously consider first completing an LLM that includes a strong research component. Good research universities encourage their students to consider their Masters degree as direct preparation for the PhD. A key point to a Masters that is preparation for a doctorate is to choose a dissertation topic that may serve as a background study for more detailed doctoral research. Another aspect of preparation concerns the subjects you choose to study (if you decide to take some taught components). As doctorates require you to engage with the theoretical underpinnings of the law, it will be worthwhile taking some theory-based subjects as part of your Masters. This doesn't necessarily mean you have to spend a year reading Aristotle, Locke, Kant, Marx and Habermas. A theoretically-engaged Masters doesn't have to be an LLM in Legal Theory. Rather, it is about choosing modules or courses that go beyond doctrinal analysis and dig a little deeper into the law. The skills that such courses teach—whether they are in the areas of constitutional or company law, tort or tax law—will help you to be a more successful doctoral student. In addition to writing a strong dissertation and choosing theoretically-engaged subjects you should also take any opportunities you are presented with to develop research skills. If you hope to conduct empirical research as part of your PhD then you will certainly benefit from appropriate methods training at Masters level. Of course, for many doctoral researchers the idea of doing a PhD only arises during the Masters degree and so it is not possible to tailor that degree for doctoral preparation. But if you happen to be planning in advance then making the right choices at Masters level can save you a lot of time and effort during your doctoral studies.

For the lawyer emerging from the world of undergraduate study, or the practitioner who is considering resuming study, there are several choices to be made before embarking on a PhD. If you are simply seeking to broaden or deepen your knowledge of particular legal subjects, then you may wish to cease your academic inquiries after a Masters degree. If you have completed a Masters degree and believe you want to further your studies—or if you think you can bypass the Masters degree stage altogether—then you may want to consider the value of a PhD.

THE VALUE OF A PhD IN LAW

At a very superficial level, there are some enjoyable perks to holding a doctorate. You have the satisfaction of knowing that you hold one of the highest qualifications in the country. You can ask your friends to call you 'Doctor' without having to worry about being expected to deal with medical emergencies. And you can replace your tired student Jane Doe debit card with a snazzy new Dr Jane Doe (hopefully with an appropriately-increased overdraft!). Notwithstanding the obvious enjoyment to be derived from these perks, embarking on a research degree simply to change your title on a bank card is obviously a fool's errand. Completing a PhD requires a high degree of motivation and dedication and so the prospective PhD candidate will need to be fully committed to their research project.

Shane was a successful practitioner in his field in a medium-sized firm. He had always enjoyed education and so he decided to begin a PhD. He registered at a nearby university for a part-time research degree on a topic close to his practice interests. However, it soon became clear that he had neither the aptitude nor inclination to complete a research degree. After a year of sporadic reading and writing his supervisor suggested they discuss Shane's progress and future plans. Shane ended up withdrawing from the programme after 15 months. His failure to complete wasn't a reflection on his intelligence or ability as a lawyer—the degree just wasn't for him. He had insufficient motivation and limited interest in the subject and so, in all likelihood, he would have been better off not starting it in the first place.

Vitae is an organisation that describes itself as 'championing the personal, professional and career development of doctoral researchers and research staff in higher education institutions and research institutes.' In a 2010 Vitae study of doctoral graduates, 78 per cent of respondents agreed that their course had been 'good value for money'. In general, satisfaction levels amongst doctoral graduates were higher than those amongst graduates of lower degrees (Vitae 2010). When asked what their motivations were for completing a PhD, the top five reasons offered by those in the social sciences (which included law) were:

— Interest in the subject (90.1 per cent)
— Interest in research (84.0 per cent)
— Desire for an academic career (51.9 per cent)
— Broaden career prospects (50.6 per cent)
— Awarded a scholarship (48.1 per cent)

Thus, the overwhelming majority of doctoral graduates began the degree due to an interest in both research and the particular subject, while roughly one out of every two graduates sought either an academic career in particular or better career options in general. Almost half of respondents had some form of scholarship to support their studies. Contrary perhaps to popular belief, only 8.4 per cent of respondents claimed to have wanted to 'postpone job hunting'. The typical doctoral graduate therefore started their PhD as a highly motivated individual for whom the intrinsic value of researching their subject was even more important than the instrumental value of having the doctorate.

A further benefit of completing a PhD is gaining experience in designing, carrying out and writing up the findings from a large research project. Most university degrees now require some kind of research project to be completed as part of the programme. However, as this project will only be part of your overall education you will only be expected to dedicate a portion of your time to it. Training may be minimal and certainly will not be equivalent to what you should receive as a doctoral candidate. A PhD allows you to dedicate three to four years of your life to a research project. The skills gained through carrying out this degree will stand you in good stead for the rest of your life.

In addition to the skills developed through the research project, completing a research degree will also allow you to become an expert in a particular area of law. This will obviously benefit your career, but if you have a passion for a particular subject it can be gratifying to become an expert in it. Reading and writing about one topic for three years requires both commitment and stamina, but the outcome is a truly deep knowledge of a particular field. One of the most common pieces of advice offered to those about to defend a thesis is to remember that you know it better than anyone else. While it's often little consolation to the worried candidate entering the exam of their life, it is quite rewarding when it's proven to be true at the end of the process.

THE PhD AND YOUR CAREER

The doctorate is an important part of the career of most PhD candidates and at least some will have set out on the PhD to further a particular career goal. This aspect of the PhD has undergone much development in recent years. In light of the benefits of a highly-skilled workforce to the economy there has been much investment in this area (though future investment was in doubt at the time of writing). Furthermore, as there are only a limited number of opportunities to work in universities and other parts of the education sector it is necessary for doctoral graduates to have skills they can bring to bear in different walks of life. Whether you have a career path in mind, or are more interested in the PhD as a learning process, it is important to think about where you want to end up afterwards. Because of the mystique of the legal profession, the role of the PhD in law in the career of the lawyer can be something of a mystery to the uninitiated. One of the authors was once asked whether the completion of his PhD would lead to his being entitled to serve as a judge? The answer, alas, is no. However, some recent research will help us to dispel the myths and better understand the career destinations of law PhD graduates.

In 2008 Vitae conducted a study into the career destinations of doctoral graduates—and the results are enlightening. The study found that between 2003 and 2007 there were 320 UK domiciled doctoral graduates in law. Almost 70 per cent of these had entered work in the UK at the time the research was carried out. Others had entered work *and* study, others again were studying and training. Only 0.5 per cent of respondents were 'believed unemployed'.

Some comparisons with other disciplines make for interesting reading. Doctoral graduates in law were the least likely cohort to be unemployed. Of those who were employed in the UK, the overwhelming majority were working in the education sector, with 56 per cent of law doctoral graduates employed as lecturers in higher education institutions. The next largest category of employers was other professions, which included the legal profession. One in 10 graduates worked in public administration. What does this mean for the prospective PhD applicant? The most likely career path upon graduation is in academia—teaching and/or researching law in a university. Other likely options include working in the public sector, or in the law and law-related professions. It's worth exploring these in a little more detail before continuing our consideration of the PhD in law.

Teaching and Researching in a University

The most obvious benefit of having a research degree in law is that it significantly increases your chances of being hired to teach law in a UK university. While having a PhD in law or a related subject is not yet listed as essential requirement in all academic job advertisements in the UK, it is increasingly difficult to launch a successful academic career without one. The work carried out by universities can be crudely divided into teaching and research and more and more law schools are requiring their academic staff to contribute to both strands of work. A good research degree provides much-needed training in the skills and techniques of advanced legal research and completion of the degree is seen as evidence that the job applicant can contribute to the school's research profile. In addition, the increasing number of applicants for teaching posts who do hold research degrees puts any candidate without a PhD at a serious disadvantage. The PhD is now being considered 'indispensible' even in areas such as tax law, company law and land law, where 'real-world' experience is often just as important to effective teaching and research (Tiley 2006).

Nonetheless, the role of a PhD in the career of a young academic may vary between jurisdictions. Writing in 2009 about the differences between European and US law schools, the European constitutional lawyer Matthias Kumm argued as follows:

> In the top US law schools, on the other hand, the ideal candidate is someone who has studied some other subject as an undergraduate for four years; studied law in a postgraduate professional degree program for three years; spent a couple of years in high-level practice, preferably including a high-level judicial clerkship; and then gone on to do a PhD not in law but in another discipline. The most obvious way to learn to engage law seriously as part of a sustained intellectual inquiry, it seems, is to learn the methodology of a discipline other than law. Conversely, the American PhD in law (the SJD or JSD) plays a negligible role in the training of academics

in elite law schools. There are perhaps as many JSD holders with tenure in the top ten American law schools as there are professors without a law degree. Both exist, but they are rare. The JSD serves primarily as a credential of value for foreigners in their home jurisdictions (particularly, aspiring academics from Israel, the Commonwealth, and perhaps South America, though, generally, not Continental Europe). In the US, law as an intellectual discipline that has its own internal point of view and methodology to be studied as part of a serious doctoral program is apparently not widely accepted. (Kumm 2009)

If one of your key reasons for obtaining a PhD is related to a desire to pursue a career in academia then it is worth examining where you want to work and what the standard career route is in that jurisdiction. Speak to the head of your law school and ask her what role she sees a research degree playing in the career of an early career academic.

Legal Practice and Beyond

Throughout this book, for the most part, we've assumed that readers are interested in pursuing a career in academia. But not all PhD graduates wanted to go into academia in the first place, and some people go into their PhDs thinking that's what they want and then realise that the skills acquired during the doctorate can be applied to a variety of careers in law.

If this applies to you, then you can use your time as a doctoral student wisely. You can also inquire as to the benefit of a PhD to your career in practice before you commit to three years of research. One place to (re)acquaint yourself with the professional side of the law is the annual university law fair, where firms and chambers come together to woo the best and brightest law students to their workplaces. Although these events are mostly targeted at undergraduates, here you can discuss your study plans with prospective employers, ascertain whether they are interested in people with postgraduate qualifications, and make some useful contacts in private practice for the future.

Another possible destination for law doctoral graduates is public administration. Law doctoral graduates may work directly for government as part of the civil service or they may work for other public bodies such as the Law Commission or the Electoral Commission. Vitae statistics indicate that one in 10 law doctoral graduates work in public administration. These are merely the most likely destinations. As we saw in the above data, doctoral graduates in law have a wide range of careers. If you are interested in exploring career options outside of academia, either before or during your PhD, you may want to consider completing an internship or engaging in consultancy.

Internships are often advertised through your university's postgraduate email lists. It's also worth looking on the websites of particular organisations you're interested in. There's usually an application form to complete and some organisations will only take interns at certain times of the year. If no formal internships are advertised, there's no harm in putting yourself forward: it may not have occurred to the organisation that an internship is a solution to their work overload problem.

Although they are usually unpaid (if you're lucky, the organisation may cover travel and lunch costs), internships are nonetheless worthwhile pursuing—the experience you gain is invaluable. Internships can open your eyes to the wide variety of ways lawyers use their skills and to what ends: monitoring companies' compliance with human rights, researching counterfeiting and piracy activities, and reporting on fair trial standards for the accused in war crimes trials are but a few examples of what's on offer. Internships usually involve working for a defined period for an organisation (usually a charity or non-governmental organisation (NGO)) on a particular project. Make sure you research the body offering the internship carefully before you apply. You don't want to be exploited for your free labour.

Maintaining some legal practice through a consultancy arrangement could be an appealing option and may offer a new career option after you graduate. One way of doing this is to see whether your firm is interested in retaining your services on an ongoing basis while you study. Another option is to keep an eye on legal recruitment websites for short-term posts in your area. These can be combined with your studies where there's a convenient breakpoint. Cold-calling can also work, but the reception of your inquiry is often dependent on the nature of the field you're involved in: if it's a field where the workflow is constant you're likely to receive a better response than one where the work ebbs and flows. Consultancies enable you to keep your legal skills fresh and your professional contacts up to date.

John had completed the first draft of his thesis when he saw an advertisement on an online legal recruitment site for a lawyer in the exact area of his thesis: 'As it was a short-term maternity cover, I thought why not? I applied and got the job. With my supervisor's blessing, I interrupted my studies for the six months of the contract. This proved to be a great decision. I sharpened up my professional skills, made lots of new contacts in my area, earned quite a bit of money, and got access to hard-to-find information that I was then able to incorporate into my thesis. Years later, I still provide legal opinions for them every so often—now as an expert!'

Exploring the options outside academic life can be a very valuable exercise in their own right too. Practical legal work can be a refreshing change from the long-term focus of the doctorate, and you generally get to practise a wider range of skills day-to-day than you do as a PhD student. The core work of a lawyer: research and writing on the law remains the same, but you can also find yourself advising clients in person, instructing counsel, drafting internal policies, presenting evidence to parliamentary committees and having conferences with barristers.

TO PhD OR NOT TO PhD?

Like the Danish prince contemplating his options you are now likely to be considering that difficult question: to PhD or not to PhD? If you've read this far and are still interested in completing a PhD in Law, there are several questions you should ask yourself:

— Why do I want to do a PhD? Would a different postgraduate degree be sufficient for my goals?
— Am I sufficiently motivated by my subject to conduct a (minimum) three-year research project?
— Have I thought about how my PhD will fit with my overall career plan?
— What do I want from my doctorate?

It's worth remembering that most doctoral graduates listed an interest in research and their particular subject as motivations for undertaking the degree. On long days in the library when you are trying to unpick the finer points of the EU Treaties or understand Raz's *Authority of Law* you'll need to be able to remind yourself why you've brought this work on yourself. Keep your goals in mind and the difficult days will be more bearable.

At this point you may have decided that the PhD isn't for you. If so, then you can return this book to the shelf on which you found it and spare yourself the anguish of three years' hard research. However, if you're still interested, you can proceed to chapter two, where we examine the questions to consider when deciding what your PhD should focus on and where and how you should complete it.

2

Preparing for the PhD

Now that you've decided to take the plunge and commit to a PhD, you need to start doing some groundwork. Preparation is the key not only to completing your PhD, but also enjoying the process along the way! Before you begin making your applications, there are several topics you need to have thought through. Having a clear idea of what the PhD is all about will improve your chances of a successful application. This chapter looks at the key questions you should be thinking about before you make an application to a PhD programme:

— What do I understand by a thesis?
— What is the topic of my PhD?
— What kind of programme do I want to enrol in?
— Where should I enrol?
— Whom should I approach as a supervisor?
— What is involved in making an application?

THE 'THESIS'

Many prospective PhD students find this the most daunting aspect of the entire process (and the same could probably be said for most students actually in the throes of a PhD). The thesis will come to shape and possibly even define your life for several years, so you need to understand what it is you are taking on right from the very beginning. So, what exactly is a PhD thesis?

Some people say simply that a PhD is a book. This is a handy answer to give at parties. But although the finished thesis will have the appearance of a book, this is not very helpful in unpicking the nature of the thesis and unravelling its mysteries. Other authors have offered definitions in relation to non-law PhDs, but these work just as well for law PhDs. For Rowena Murray the thesis is 'an integrated argument that can stand up to critique' (Murray 2006). Patrick Dunleavy defines it as 'the development and communication of a question to which one proffers an answer' (Dunleavy 2003). A more detailed definition comes from the Quality Assurance Agency for Higher Education, the body responsible for auditing higher education institutions in the UK. Its framework of academic qualifications says the following about PhDs:

> Doctorates are awarded to students who have demonstrated:
>
> (a) the creation and interpretation of new knowledge, through original research or other advanced scholarship, of a quality to satisfy peer review, extend the forefront of the discipline, and merit publication;
> (b) a systematic acquisition and understanding of a substantial body of knowledge which is at the forefront of an academic discipline or area of professional practice;
> (c) the general ability to conceptualise, design and implement a project for the generation of new knowledge, applications or understanding at the forefront of the discipline, and to adjust the project design in the light of unforeseen problems;
> (d) a detailed understanding of applicable techniques for research and advanced academic enquiry. (QAA 2001)

It is clear from this definition that the doctorate concerns the creation of new knowledge through a rigorous process of research and reporting. For a further definition, a good, and for lawyers, a happily familiar, place to start is with the degree regulations for the institution you want to apply to. For example, the University of London PhD regulations state that the thesis shall:

> (a) consist of the candidate's own account of her investigations, the greater proportion of which shall have been undertaken during the period of registration under supervision for the degree;
> (b) and form a distinct contribution to knowledge of the subject and afford evidence of originality by the discovery of new facts and/or by the exercise of independent critical power;
> (c) and be an integrated whole and present a coherent argument;
> (d) and give a critical assessment of the relevant literature, describe the method of research and its findings, include discussion of those findings and indicate in which respects they appear to the candidate to advance the study of the subject, demonstrate a deep and synoptic understanding of the field of study, objectivity and capacity for judgment in complex situations and autonomous work in the field; .....
> (e) and not exceed 100 000 words;
> (f) and be of a standard to merit publication in whole or in part or in a revised form.

Note the key aspects of this definition: the thesis is your own work forming a distinct contribution to the knowledge of the subject, either by the discovery of new facts and/or by the exercise of independent critical power, being a complete and coherent piece of work within the current literature of the field. Meeting these criteria can seem intimidating, especially at the beginning of the doctorate. Let's break this down.

First, the thesis has to be your own work. Simply summarising or repeating the work of others will not do. Secondly, this work has to be a distinct contribution to the knowledge of the subject. This means that you have to bring something fresh and new to the discipline. What are you planning to do that is different? Note that doing something different can be done in many different and small ways—we consider these further in chapter four. Next, *how* have you carved out your own niche with this new piece of work? This is the key criterion of originality. At this stage, it's enough to say that originality can be achieved in two main ways: by the discovery of new facts, or, more likely in the case of a law doctorate, by showing the application of independent critical power to the topic of your thesis. So you should be thinking about the analytical contribution you will make to the material or phenomena you are researching, perhaps by bringing in a new perspective, by suggesting possible law reforms, or solving a particular legal puzzle. Your work also has to be complete and coherent: your argument must present as a whole with no loose ends or stray arguments, and it must be clear and understandable. Lastly, your work has to find its place within the discipline, showing where it sits in relation to the current literature—in law, this means not only texts and scholarly articles, but also the international or domestic legislative framework or the jurisprudence of any relevant courts or international governance bodies.

CHOOSING A PhD TOPIC

When faced with the prospect of spending three years or more studying the same topic, your first priority must be to choose a topic that interests you. Picking a topic that you think will guarantee you a job or make your reputation in the legal world or even one which is simply fashionable at the moment, but which you don't have any real desire to study is more likely to ensure that you don't finish.

Some people begin their PhDs with a topic already presented to them; the topic comes to them, rather than the other way round. This is more likely in the case of a PhD studentship where funding is allocated by a research council or university to support the investigation of a particular topic under the guidance of a named supervisor. Some examples at the time of writing this chapter, as advertised on the website www.jobs.ac.uk, include a four-year post as a doctoral researcher in international law and human rights law from the Centre for Global Governance Studies of the Katholieke Universiteit Leuven and a three-year doctoral research post in charity law at the University of Liverpool. Joining a group project is something to be carefully considered. On the one hand, you have the security of knowing that there will be other people researching in your area and therefore you are sure to have a community with which to discuss your work. On the other hand unless the project is based in an area which interests you you may struggle to remain interested in the topic throughout the doctorate. Thus, it might be best only to get involved in a group project if the area is one you are passionate about.

More common in the world of the law PhD is the self-selected topic. If your topic is to be self-selected you will settle on the research idea first and then choose an institution and supervisor. Of course, occasionally a student will be so keen to study under a particular supervisor that the choice of topic will be negotiated between the two parties. We know of one now quite renowned jurist whose doctoral thesis was in an area entirely unrelated to his current work as that was the only topic his supervisor, a leading lawyer in the twentieth century, was willing to supervise.

You might of course already have a good idea of what you want to be the subject of your thesis. Perhaps you want to develop an idea you encountered during your LLM or LLB studies, but didn't have the time or opportunity to take further. Perhaps a recent development in the law or world elsewhere has captured your attention. Perhaps a particular period of legal history or a particular law has always fascinated you. Passion for the subject matter will stand you in good stead when progress is slow.

On the other hand, if you want to start afresh with your PhD, then cast your net as wide as possible. Don't discount possible topics just because you are not familiar with their finer details. Think about the subjects that really captured your attention during law school—what classes did you look forward to? Which subjects did you want to know more about? Have you encountered a perspective on the law, such as law and economics, that you want to apply to a specific topic? You can look through recent editions of law reviews to see if anything sparks your interest; the popular or legal press can also be a fruitful source of new ideas to research—sometimes a legal problem will manifest itself in practice long before it comes to the attention of the courts or academics. Your former lecturers might also be a useful channel of inquiry (although don't expect them to formulate a PhD topic for you!).

Are your interests in a particular area, such as criminal responsibility, or financial regulation? Within that area, is there a question you have burning inside you, such as what underlies the different ages for the criminal responsibility of minors in different countries, or what is the potential for improving the legal framework addressing international cooperation in money-laundering? Keep on asking yourself these questions until you find yourself coming back to the same idea again and again.

Chris had decided to apply to a PhD programme but was having difficulty settling on a topic. He was drafting a short research proposal but found himself lacking any real enthusiasm—hardly a good sign if he was going to have to research the topic for three long years. Inspiration came in a predictable if still unexpected form. Chris attended an afternoon seminar at which one of his course lecturers was speaking. While the seminar focussed on a single case it grabbed Chris' attention. He did some further reading into the area of UK public law in question and was surprised to find that despite there being inter-esting questions in the field there was relatively little research being conducted. He had, at last, found his PhD topic.

Once you have a topic in mind, some preliminary research will be needed. Most law schools and funding bodies will require you to provide a formal research proposal of about 2,000 words as part of your application. This does not need to be a full outline of everything you hope to accomplish in your PhD studies, but it does need to show the school and your potential supervisor that you have a good understanding of the research question to be investigated, that you have an ultimate goal and purpose to your study, an understanding of the research methodology you propose to adopt, and an awareness of the current literature in the area and where your proposed work fits into this. You may also be required to set out a timeline for the various stages of your research. You need to have done enough work to be able to set all this out in the application.

As part of this stage, you will probably find it helpful to approach potential supervisors or other academics in the area that interests you. They should be able to point you to helpful sources of information you might not have considered, ask you questions that will push along the development of your topic, and give you an idea of whether your topic is sustainable as a doctoral thesis or not. This is a useful process for working out the boundaries of your topic and one you might need to repeat a number of times as you conduct your preliminary research. Research is an iterative process—it's rare that you will arrive at a complete answer the first time you set out to investigate some-thing, so this is good preparation for doctoral study.

Your actual thesis topic, that is, the question you want to answer or the field you want to investigate, is likely to still be quite broad at this initial stage. Don't be too concerned with pinning down every single aspect of your studies before you have even begun. You will find that it changes at different stages of the PhD programme.

Sometimes the change will come about through the twists and turns of the research journey. You might start off thinking that you want to look at how the law relating to surrogacy arrangements deals with the fundamental con-cepts of contract law, and discover along the way that you are more interested in the dispute resolution processes that govern disagreements in surrogacy contracts. Or you might begin your studies wanting to examine the role of inquiries in the constitution generally and then narrow down your research into looking at the impact of one particular inquiry. Or you might want to look at extradition treaties between two particular nations and, as you find that the problems they experience are widespread, expand your studies to cover a number of jurisdictions.

Jane began researching quite a broad PhD topic—the effect of criminal justice legislation in the 2000s on civil liberties in Britain. Her supervisor encouraged her to spend some time at the outset of the degree reading around her subject to see if she could pinpoint a more precise research topic. Over time she realised that she could. Her specific interest was the manner in which criminal justice had become to be used as a solution to social problems such as anti-social behaviour and the resulting impact on individual rights. It took several weeks of reading academic literature to arrive at that more focussed research topic. This is to be expected; while Jane was aware of some literature in the area she only developed a more full understanding of the academic and policy debates once she had started researching. This process allowed her to turn her 'hunch' into a fully-fledged research question.

Sometimes the introduction of new statutes, developments in case law, or political events can themselves change the nature of your topic—be prepared for this, and be flexible enough to adapt your thesis to accommodate these external changes. Being too proscriptive about what your research is about or where it is going can stop it in its tracks when it meets an unforeseen development.

One way to think about the boundaries and content of your topic is to imagine what the eventual title of the thesis might be. It doesn't need to be a clever pun or a topical reference (in fact, this is a short-cut to dating your thesis and it could even cloud what your thesis is about). The thesis title should convey the general thrust and limits of the thesis, which might be jurisdictional, geographical, temporal or conceptual, and do so clearly and immediately. Here are some examples from recently completed and in progress theses:

— The Role, Nature, and Reform of the Law Regulating Westminster Parliamentary Candidacy and Membership
— The Development of Retirement Pensions in the United Kingdom: 1908–2008
— Street Art, Graffiti and the Counter-Regulation of Public Space
— The WTO: An Organisation for Development through Trade
— Peace and Unquiet—Integrating Routes of Justice in Post-Conflict Sierra Leone

TYPES OF PhD PROGRAMME

UK PhDs

In many UK law schools, the doctoral programme consists of three years of independent study culminating in a piece of writing of about 100,000 words. Students can enter the doctoral programme after completing an LLM, or in some cases, you may be allowed to enrol if you have a very high quality LLB. In some law schools, the first year of enrolment will be spent in a research Masters programme which then counts towards the PhD if you decide to go forward with your doctoral studies.

Less common is what is known as the '1+3' model or the four-year PhD. In this type of programme your first year consists of advanced skills and research training after which you progress to the traditional three-year programme. Is it also possible to leave with a Masters degree if you decide to leave the programme at this point.

You will need to decide when applying for a place on a PhD programme whether you want to pursue the degree on a part- or full-time basis. The choice between a part-time or full-time PhD very much depends on your own personal circumstances and restrictions. The default position is three years (or some-times four) of full-time enrolment on the PhD programme, but that does not mean that completing a PhD on a part-time basis can't be done. In a part-time programme, you will usually proceed at half the expected pace of the full-time programme, taking six years rather than three years to complete. While many doctoral programmes are flexible enough to allow you to change between full-time and part-time status should the need arise, some institutions will only offer the degree on a full-time basis. Whichever route you take it is important to have a research plan that is realistic about how much time you can spend on your project.

Other Jurisdictions

The law PhD in the US is known as the SJD or JSD (Doctor of Juridical Science), to distinguish it from the first law degree, the JD. Many US law schools make enrolment in their LLM programmes a requirement for applying to the SJD.

In some law schools, the SJD is awarded on the basis of written work only. There are two ways of satisfying this requirement. One is identical to the tra-ditional UK law PhD, requiring the production of a thesis (known in the US as a dissertation) after several years of independent study. Another way is by writing three separate articles, each of significant length and capable of being the lead article in a law review. If the second route is chosen, then the three articles usually have to be accompanied by a prefatory piece that identifies the common theme or general thesis in the articles. Some law schools offer both options, others only the dissertation option.

Other law schools offer SJD programmes which are a combination of coursework and writing. This shares some similarities with the new 1+3 model in the UK. The coursework is undertaken first. In some schools the coursework is selected from the options offered to LLM students, while in others, students compile their own programme from a combination of independent reading based around certain themes and coursework. Another difference in some US SJD programmes is that you may not have a sole supervisor, but instead a dissertation committee of three or four academics who will assess your work.

You may be considering doing your PhD in another European country, particularly if your research interests are comparative or international in nature. While you may think that this requires you to be fluent in another language, many European institutions have the capacity to allow you to write your thesis and be examined in English, while at the same time exposing you to a different intellectual and cultural environment. This is particularly the case with pan-European institutions such as the European University Institute and the Central European University. In some PhD programmes, this is actually a requirement!

The huge range of institutions and jurisdictions offering doctoral programmes in law across Europe make it difficult to give any specific advice about what you might expect if you embark on this journey. You will need to check the regulations for the particular institution you are thinking of applying to. However, in general law PhDs in Europe are not markedly different from what you might experience in the UK or the US. This is unsurprising since (as we noted in chapter one) the very first modern PhD was awarded in Germany by the Friedrich Wilhelm University in the early 1800s. So you will probably find yourself choosing between the traditional thesis model, or the 1+3 model of seminars (either a structured set programme or one more individually tailored to your research project) followed by the writing of the thesis.

Jasmine was a Canadian student who decided to study international trade law in Germany: 'After completing my LLM in the UK I decided to undertake my doctorate on the Continent. A large part of this decision was based on lifestyle factors: I wanted to experience life outside the Anglo-American culture I was used to, learn a new language and improve upon the food and coffee I had dealt with in England! Germany has delivered on all those fronts. Travel opportunities also featured prominently in my decision—the ability to grab cheap rail fares all around Germany and neighbouring countries has been a big plus. Academically it has been very satisfying to experience the Continental academic and legal tradition. I am able to study and write in English, and I have been given access to excellent resources in terms of office and library facilities. I also have a generous stipend. The downside of the German system is that with so many doctoral students there is very little supervision or direction—I just have to "write a book" of no fixed word limit, and if I can finish in under 3 years this will be encouraged. By focussing on an international area I have kept my study relevant for later years, but I am also taking every opportunity to attend comparative discussions and talks on European topics that are giving me a better insight into "the civilians" and their way of thinking about the law.'

Remember that where you complete your PhD may play an important part in shaping your career—academic or otherwise. So do give the matter some thought before jumping at the first opportunity that comes your way!

CHOOSING AN INSTITUTION AND SUPERVISOR

There is no right answer as to how you should make your choice when it comes to the question of where to apply. However, it is important to bear in mind that where you studied and who your supervisor is will often be taken as a shorthand indicator of the quality of your degree. Some people choose the institution first, and then look for a suitable supervisor. If you take this route, you have to make sure that there is a suitable supervisor for your topic, and it is less likely that you will get the 'perfect' supervisor in terms of expertise and research interests. Others choose the supervisor first, and apply to the law school where that person is based. Remember that some academics can be based at more than one law school (splitting their time between the UK and the US, or the UK and Europe) and also that the leader in a particular field may not always be at the leading university.

Institutions

Many academics will advise you that you should study for your PhD at a different institution from the one at which you gained your undergraduate or masters degree. Changing institutions exposes you to a new research community, new ideas, and different ways of doing things. However, this is not always possible. Family or work commitments or sometimes, a particularly attractive doctoral programme or funding package, can keep your choices small or non-existent. If this is your situation, then focus your efforts on getting the very best supervisor available.

If you are in a position to choose, there are a number of factors to take into account. First, what is the research orientation of the law school (if any)? Is it known for its socio-legal approach? Is it a black letter school whose scholarship focuses on doctrinal work? Does it produce philosophers or practitioners, or both? The type and fit of the school with your intended research project is an important consideration. How many academics are working in the area you want to pursue for your thesis? Will you have a choice of supervisor, or is there only one person suitable?

Secondly, what is the reputation of the school or university? You probably already have an idea of where your preferred law school ranks, but if not, these days you can quickly get an idea of a law school's relative standing from the various 'league tables' published by newspapers, the main ones being the

Times and the *Guardian's* rankings. Be aware though, that these rankings are based on a number of criteria, some of which may not be relevant to your doctorate. A more research-focussed ranking comes from the REF (formerly the RAE) exercise. REF stands for Research Excellence Framework and aims to produce an assessment on three fronts of an institution's research activities. These are: the quality of the research outputs; their impact; and the vitality of the research environment. Of course these rankings are not set in stone and a lot can happen at an institution in the space of a few years; you should not discount a school that fits all your other criteria simply on the basis of its REF ranking. In addition, you should remember that there may be a difference between the REF ranking and the treatment given to doctoral researchers—it is the latter that should be your principal concern.

Thirdly, what are the general research facilities of the law school like? This is not such an issue in the age of electronic databases, where the need for a well-stocked law library is not so critical, but it still needs investigating. In some cases your own law school's library might not be so important if you have access to a library like that of the Institute of Advanced Legal Studies, or you use the SCONUL Access scheme to borrow from other law schools' libraries. You should also think about whether you intend to use any specialist librar-ies as part of your research and whether your university offers easy access to them.

Another factor to consider in your choice of institution is the support available to PhD students. This can make a real difference to your experience. If the institution offers good support to its students—including both intellec-tual and pastoral guidance—then you are much more likely to have a positive doctoral experience. No two institutions are the same so asking around in advance is the best way to find out what you can expect.

Fraser discovered that his law department did not pay much attention to the non-academic side of doing a PhD: 'I found the university and the law department very good at academic support but not that good on the emotional side. There are lots of structures and offices to help you if you have academic problems but not much that helps with the emotional impact of doing a PhD, especially if you have health issues. Some kind of mentor or buddy system alongside supervision might have helped but this was lacking in my department.'

Some questions to investigate are:

— Is there dedicated administrative support for PhD students?
— Is there a dedicated law librarian?
— Is there a member of academic staff responsible for PhD students?
— Does the law school or university provide research training for PhD students?
— Are there opportunities to present my work?
— Are there research clusters in the school I can join to discuss my work with other students or academics?

— Do PhD students have office space within the law school? Is it individual or shared? What is the quality of the accommodation like?
— What other sorts of facilities are available for PhDs? Is there printing? Photocopying? Is it free? What about IT resources?
— What sort of funding is available to PhDs, for example, for conference attendance or research materials?
— Are there any opportunities to gain teaching experience while studying?
— What is the PhD student community like? Is there one? Can I speak to some current students?

Nathan gives a word of warning about what to look for when investigating PhD programmes: 'The postgraduate community in my department is rather quiet. The PhD students have very few opportunities to meet academics and discuss their research. Unlike other university departments I've experienced, there's a strong hierarchical division between students and staff, with the result that PhD students are not really part of the research community. I overcame this isolation by attending reading and discussion groups connected to my research run by other departments.'

Supervisor

Choosing the right supervisor is crucial to the success of your PhD programme. An uninterested or lazy supervisor can add years to your time studying; an interested and engaged supervisor can keep you feeling motivated and positive about your work, and more likely to finish. A supervisor will also be in your life for many years after the PhD, writing references for jobs and fellowships, and acting as an older and wiser academic mentor, so choose carefully. Choosing a supervisor (if you are in a position to do this—you may find that the law school simply informs you who your supervisor will be) essentially comes down to two things: expertise and the nature of the supervisor.

If you have reached the stage of putting together a proposal and having spent many years in law school already, you should have a good idea of who the leading figures in your field are, and whom you would like to approach to act as a supervisor. You should begin, if you haven't already, by reading the work of your potential supervisors. This should give you a feel for their approach to their subject, their favourite themes, and their bugbears. Check how these match up with what you are hoping to do. There is a little point in having the greatest name in the field as a supervisor if you know from day one that she is implacably opposed to your proposed methodology.

If you haven't done so already by this stage, you should be approaching potential supervisors informally (most likely by email) to sound out their views on your proposed research. This can be a very worthwhile exercise—you do not want to find out that your preferred supervisor is not really interested in your topic only after you've been accepted into the programme. You might also learn some things that you might not otherwise discover, such as an impending retirement or long-term research leave plans that would mean your losing a supervisor halfway through.

A word of caution about experts or 'academic celebrities': it is tempting to go for the biggest name in your field, thinking that the more senior and renowned the supervisor, the more of that gloss will rub off on you. Perhaps it might. But remember also that people who have become big names have many other demands on their time; you may find that you are not a priority amongst the calls from government to advise on legislation, NGOs or law firms seeking expert advice, making keynote conference addresses and the academic's own work. Think carefully about the amount of time and support a supervisor might be able to offer you. A more junior academic (who could still be reasonably senior without being an academic superstar) may well have more time and enthusiasm for your thesis.

As well as the supervisor's expertise, you should also do some thinking about what kind of supervisor you might need. What sort of student are you and what sort of role are you hoping the supervisor will play in your PhD?

Are you looking for an active supervisor, the sort of person who will set deadlines and then prod you to meet them? Or are you the kind of student who is looking for a more laidback supervisor who will leave it up to you to get the work done? Both types are equally valid; the kind you will benefit most from will depend on your own working style. Think also about the qualities you are looking for in a supervisor: a fierce critic, a friendly advisor, an avuncular mentor, a methodical manager? The supervisor's personality is also very important in determining the nature of the supervisory relationship.

Some supervisors approach the role on a strictly professional basis: they will read your work, provide critique, and further reading suggestions or avenues of research, all the while keeping their distance from the non-thesis aspects of your life. Your only contact with your supervisor might be in his office. Others will take a more involved or informal approach—you may find yourself have a supervision session in a café that covers not just your thesis, but ranges over other aspects of your life as well.

If you can, try meeting with potential supervisors. This will help you judge whether the supervisor is someone you can get on with and trust over the course of your PhD studies. Someone who looks perfect on paper may turn out to be not so perfect in person. Also helpful, if you are in a position to do this, is to talk to other students that person is supervising—they can be very valuable sources of information!

Desmond applied to two institutions for his doctoral degree. One was the institution in which he had completed his LLM and the other was another university, Elsewhere College, of similar standing in the same city. When invited to interview at Elsewhere College, Desmond found that his prospective supervisor in that university was quite enthusiastic about his project. The programme director was very welcoming and he was treated more as a colleague than as a student. While the facilities were comparable at both institutions the better treatment he received at Elsewhere convinced him to switch institution. The university's attitude to doctoral researchers, something he could not have judged on paper, swung his decision. He has since begun part-time teaching at Elsewhere College and believes his decision has been vindicated by his experience at Elsewhere.

Remember—the support you receive from both the supervisor and the wider school environment will be key to deciding how (and sometimes if) you complete your doctorate. We know of individuals who have obtained their PhDs despite their supervisor, but it's much more enjoyable to do so with the help and support of someone you trust.

MAKING YOUR APPLICATION

There are usually two stages to making an application to a PhD programme. As we've noted, there is quite a bit of preliminary work to do before setting pen to paper (or more likely these days, logging in to the university's online application form). You need to have thought about the university you would like to attend, have approached one or more potential supervisors, and have drafted up a research proposal. Don't underestimate the time that the whole application process can take. If you want to begin a research degree in September of a particular year you should realistically start investigating your options in the preceding autumn or winter.

The first step will usually be to approach an expert in the field in which you study to see if he or she is willing to supervise your project. There's no one right way to approach a potential supervisor, but there are some things you can do to increase your chances of piquing an academic's interest and so getting accepted. Be concise and to the point. Briefly set out your educational background (perhaps a line on your undergraduate degree and one on any postgraduate degrees or professional qualifications), explain in a few sentences the research you'd like to pursue and why you think the academic you're contacting would be a suitable supervisor. Avoid flattery and don't try to glide over any potential troublesome points.

Although you will probably have to draft a research proposal at some point in the admissions process, there are pros and cons to including it in the initial approach to a supervisor. On the one hand, attaching a research proposal to an initial proposal demonstrates that you're serious about the research. On the other hand, a potential supervisor may take longer to reply to correspondence that encloses a research proposal (as they will want to read it and consider it in more detail). This may slow down the process of finding someone willing to supervise your work, especially if you are kept waiting only to find out that they're not interested. On balance, it may be best to send a short informal inquiry first and follow up with a research proposal if the academic is interested. It may well be that you will want to apply to more than one university. If so, you should contact a different academic in each institution, making sure to tailor your inquiry in each case.

The actual formal application will typically involve an application form to which you will be expected to attach your research proposal. You are likely to be asked for your grades from your undergraduate and any relevant post-graduate degrees as well as for information relating to how you are going to fund your research. In most cases, the three most important parts of the application are your academic record, your research proposal and your academic references. Approach the form with the same professionalism you would an important job application. Universities receive hundreds of applications a year and can afford to be choosy.

There is little you can do on an application form to dress up your existing academic record—and so it is important to make the research proposal as attractive as possible to the university to which you are applying. Demonstrate that you are aware of existing research in your field, show how the research relates to work you have already completed and make clear the ways in which your work could contribute to the research culture in your target department. This is essentially the PhD student's equivalent of a job application, so try to make it the best it can possibly be. While your research is likely to evolve during the course of the project, a good initial proposal will demonstrate the key skills of a doctoral researcher—the ability to critically engage with literature, to develop academic arguments at the highest level, and to present your thoughts in a clear and concise fashion. Even if the project that you embark upon ends up being entirely different, exhibiting these skills will attract the eye of both your potential supervisor and the admissions tutor.

It is also possible to exert a certain degree of influence over the third important part of the admissions paperwork: your references. Good references can encourage an admissions tutor to give a second look to a borderline candidate, while bad references can be the end of an application. To ensure your references help rather than hinder your application, choose your referees very carefully. Unless there are very good reasons not to do so (such as returning to university after a long period of employment), you should have at least one and ideally two academic referees. Put simply, this means two people who hold academic positions and are willing to comment on your academic record. The referees will need to be aware of any research work you have carried out in the past (be sure to draw it to their attention) and thus a dissertation supervisor is often an ideal referee. The best references also comment on the research proposal and how it relates to your previous work, so you should discuss the proposal with your referees before asking them to write you a reference. Finally, some referees write better references than others. Sometimes good candidates come with references that do not present them in the best light. This may be because the referee does not know the candidate as well as they should but in some instances it is simply because the referee has not put the time into writing a decent recommendation. While an admissions tutor should identify a lazy reference as precisely that and discount it you will have lost the opportunity to impress on this front. If you can make discreet inquiries before asking an academic to act as referee this may help your choice.

Having completed the application form and put the finishing touches to your research proposal, try to leave it for at least 24 hours before submitting. Typographical errors and the like detract from an application and you are more likely to spot these with fresh eyes than you are immediately after writing the application. If possible, ask friends or colleagues to review your application to make sure everything is clear and precise. Finally, before you submit the application ensure that you have provided all the information asked for, otherwise you are likely to slow the application process down. If there is any information or documentation you are unable to provide make this clear on the form—and explain when you will be able to forward it.

Once you submit your application you will inevitably have to endure something of a wait. Some institutions may invite you to interview before making a final decision. You may be interviewed by an admissions tutor, an expert in the field (most likely your prospective supervisor), or both. At the interview stage the university is trying to confirm that you are a good fit for the department and that if admitted, you are likely to complete the programme successfully. Many of the tips that apply to job interviews also apply here. One difference in an academic interview is that you will need to be willing to admit that you don't know everything. It will greatly help your case if you yourself point out any weaknesses in your proposal and explain how you intend to address these problems. Be confident but be willing to take on board any suggestions from the interviewers. Remember, even if you don't gain admission at one particular institution, the advice you get may help you improve your research in the future. The interview is likely to be the final stage in the admissions process and hopefully you will be successful!

One final point is worth noting. Admissions are increasingly linked to scholarship applications and may be conditional on your securing funding and/or attaining certain grades in any degrees you are yet to finish. Try to have a backup plan in case your plans fall through: either a second institution to which you have applied or another way to spend your time if you do not start a PhD. By doing so you demonstrate to the admissions tutor that you are capable of planning ahead and you put yourself under less pressure throughout the whole process.

THE F-WORD (FUNDING)

A January 2011 article in *The Guardian* newspaper somewhat glumly asked 'who can afford a doctorate in the arts and humanities now?' The current state of university funding—across the world but particularly in the UK—has resulted in there being less funding available for research outside of the STEM subjects: science, technology, engineering and mathematics. While there is still some funding available for those doing doctorates in other subjects such as the social sciences and arts and humanities (both categories can be considered to include law), thinking about funding needs to be done early if you are to have any hope of success. When you are putting together your grand research project, don't get so caught up in your plans that you neglect to think about who is going to pay for the PhD. Doctoral fees can amount to tens of thousands of pounds over the course of your degree and more than one PhD hopeful has been put off by the cost involved. Others have found their studies derailed or indefinitely postponed as the money runs out. Fees are only part of the picture. You will also need to think about the associated costs of studying—books, computer and printing equipment—as well as general living costs. Tempting though the thought may be, you cannot live in a tent constructed out of draft chapters and eat old journal articles.

That said, what are your options for funding? The golden ticket to funding a PhD is a studentship that covers both fees and your maintenance costs for the duration of your studies (usually for three years). Investigate funding opportunities at the universities you are thinking of applying to. More and more universities are offering studentships which pay your fees and/or a living allowance. Sometimes this funding is available simply in return for you registering at the university but in other cases you will have to do some teaching or research assistance work to earn the fees and stipend. A studentship takes the pressure off having to find a large lump sum for fees at the beginning of the academic year, allows you to keep a reasonable standard of living while at the same time enabling you to gain that all-important teaching experience. Details should be on the university website or the administrator responsible for law PhDs should be able to help you.

Funding bodies are another alternative. These can range from national research councils such as the Arts and Humanities Research Council to small charities. Funding is sometimes tailored to specific groups such as women, or people from a particular country or region. The more specific the group, the less competition there is likely to be, so don't overlook the smaller grants on offer. Funding bodies may offer grants that cover all of your fees and living expenses, or you may be able to stitch together several different grants from a range of bodies. A list of some of these funding bodies can be found in Appendix B at the back of this book. Don't forget the deadlines—you may have to apply well over a year in advance especially if you are applying from abroad and you do not fit into the UK academic year timetable.

The timetable for applying can also present difficulties if you want to move straight from your Masters degree into a doctorate. If competition is tough you may not be able to secure a studentship without having your postgraduate degree results available for the consideration of the awarding body. However, these results will (obviously) only be available once you have concluded your degree. As a result it is not unusual for good candidates to take a one-year break between the Masters degree and beginning the doctorate—it is often the best way to maximise one's chances of securing a scholarship. If you do go for this option try not to see this as time wasted. Time out between the taught and research degrees can also help you to build up some 'real-world' experience in your field and maybe even earn some money. And if taking the year helps you secure a scholarship then it's almost certainly going to save you time in the long run as you won't have to juggle jobs and your thesis.

A further funding option is relying on monies that you have accumulated yourself. These might come from savings or you might be hoping to pay your fees by working during your studies. Or perhaps family members have offered to support you. Think carefully before relying on either of these two options. Ask yourself whether you have calculated the amount you'll need (and bear in mind that funding will be required for quite a few years so don't underestimate the amount) and whether family relationships can bear the strain of supporting you as you engage in your research. Working while studying can be done but take care that work doesn't prevent you from making progress—it may be easy to put off work on that chapter for another day, but the demands of the workplace are not so easily postponed. If you do work during your studies, try to find work that will enhance your CV—either tutoring or legal work in same area as your research. The latter in particular can sometimes open your eyes to cutting-edge legal problems or other perspectives that you might be able to incorporate into your research.

CONCLUSION

At this point you should have a fairly good idea of how to go about finding the PhD programme that is right for you. The key factors are likely to be:

— Location: where the university is based;
— Supervision: whether there is an expert available or not;
— Funding: can you obtain a scholarship;
— Community: whether you will you have adequate support.

Each consideration will have different weighting depending on your personal circumstances. In the next chapter we begin to consider the research itself—as we examine different legal research methodologies.

3

Legal Research Methodologies

In this chapter we begin to unpack one of the key aspects of a PhD. A doctoral programme essentially boils down to two main activities: research and writing (procrastination in the first two coming an unofficial third). This chapter examines a fundamental part of the research process: the selection and application of a legal research methodology.

Unlike social science or physical sciences degrees, undergraduate, and to a large extent, Masters, degrees in law do not provide much by way of formal training in research methods or methodologies, other than the dominant doctrinal approach to thinking and writing about law. Even this may have been mostly by osmosis; it is just 'what lawyers do'. And your exposure to other perspectives on law may be quite limited, especially if you have not taken any classes in jurisprudence, legal philosophy or the history of legal thought.

Consequently, many doctoral students come to this aspect of their studies with some trepidation, wondering what methodology is, and how to best use it to enhance their research project. Do not be tempted to bury your head in the sand and hope that the whole issue of methodology will go away. Methodology is very important! The questions we investigate here are:

— Why is methodology important?
— What methodologies are there?
— How do I go about choosing a methodology?
— How do I develop a research project around a methodology?

The *Oxford English Dictionary* defines 'methodology' as follows:

> Originally: the branch of knowledge that deals with method generally or with the methods of a particular discipline or field of study; (arch.) a treatise or dissertation on method; (Bot.) †systematic classification (obs. rare). Subsequently also: the study of the direction and implications of empirical research, or of the suitability of the techniques employed in it; (more generally) a method or body of methods used in a particular field of study or activity.

It is the final use of the term that is most relevant to our discussion. In this chapter we use the term 'methodology' to refer to the particular way or ways in which you carry out your research, and also to any accompanying assumptions and perspectives, articulated or not, surrounding an investigation into a research topic. If you decide to conduct research into the history of laws regulating the ability to strike, will you be framing your research with a libertarian or Marxist perspective, or something else? There may also be rules stemming from your chosen method which will shape your research investigations. If you are investigating prison reform laws will you carry out personal interviews with prisoners, government officials and prison staff, or will you be looking at the written record of statutes and government reports only? Or will you use a combination of the two?

Clearly, the methodology you adopt can have quite an impact on how your research is carried out, but be aware that it can also affect what you find and are able to present. This in turn will affect the arguments you make in your thesis and the conclusions you reach. Each of these factors needs to be considered quite early in the research process so you do not commit to a methodology that is unsuited to the project you are trying to carry out.

THE IMPORTANCE OF METHODOLOGY

Your methodology is crucially important—it provides the structure and underpinnings both to your research and to your arguments based on your research. Articulating the methodology you've employed also makes it clear what your particular scholarly perspective is; this helps others to understand where you are coming from in your work, and where your work sits in relation to that of others. Even if you think you do not have a methodology, that you are just 'doing research', you will have a way of conducting your research and thinking about the legal arguments that is determined at least in part by your life experiences and position in society (this is in fact known as 'standpoint epistemology').

We've referred to methodology here but actually there are many methodologies, and schools within those methodologies that you may choose from to strengthen and guide your work. There is no one right methodology or perfect methodology and you may find that your work incorporates one or more methodologies depending on the nature and needs of your research.

Andrew's research into sentencing is mostly theory based, but it also has some practical aspects: 'One aspect of my research is to examine restorative justice as an alternative to custodial sentences and consider the justifications for punishment it relies on. I will be carrying out interviews with judges, magistrates and practitioners to get their perspectives as to what sentencing is, or should be aimed at. I will also be carrying out observations of restorative justice conferences and interviewing the participants. I chose this approach to ensure my research has a practical grounding.'

We recommend thinking about methodology at a very early stage, preferably when putting together your initial proposal. This will save you a lot of trouble later—it is better to work your research around your methodology than the other way round. You may have a grounding in other disciplines which means you are familiar with a particular type of research methodology, or perhaps a variety. But many law PhD students often do not have research methods training as part of their earlier degrees, or they absorb a research method unconsciously during their studies, and are thus unaware that their thinking and writing are shaped by certain perspectives and rules. Whatever your situation, take some time before you begin your studies to think about how you are going to conduct your research. And, if your law school offers training in legal research methodologies as part of your doctoral programme, we recommend that you take advantage of it at the earliest opportunity.

TYPES OF LEGAL RESEARCH METHODOLOGIES

Writing in 2007, McConville and Chui noted that they could not, in a single book, hope to discuss all legal research methodologies (McConville and Chui 2007). It goes without saying therefore that we cannot, in a single chapter, analyse the entire range of legal methodologies or treat each one in the depth it deserves. What we have aimed to do instead is to provide an introduction to some of the major types of legal methodology. From here you can investigate further those which interest you.

Legal methodologies fall into two broad categories. There are first, those which are internally-focused: that is, they look at the law as a self-contained entity. The second type of methodology is an applied or integrated methodology: it takes the insights or approach of another discipline (economics, anthropology or politics, for example) and uses them when investigating a legal problem (McConville and Chui 2007). Of course, these categories of methodologies are not mutually exclusive; you will probably find that your completed research employs a number of different approaches and methods, even if one is more in evidence than the others.

Another way of thinking about methodological approaches is that some methodologies are analytical in nature; they try to show what the law is, or why the law is the way it is; other methodologies are prescriptive, seeking to critique and reform it the law according to a particular viewpoint or set of principles.

Black Letter or Doctrinal Analysis

Doctrinal analysis is the traditional legal methodology. In its purest form it does not subscribe to any overarching theoretical perspective, nor does it concern itself with policy interests. Instead, the black letter method focuses almost entirely on law's own language of statutes and case law to make sense of the legal world. Law is seen as a self-contained system which is politically neutral and independent of other academic disciplines.

The role of the black letter lawyer is to bring consistency and coherence to a set of rules that might appear at first glance to be an unrelated or jumbled mass. This aim is premised on the idea that the law is based on certain principles, which can be revealed through studying the relevant laws. Once the premise is discerned, such as the protection of private property, the free will of individuals, or a concern for the welfare of children, then the law can be assessed for compliance with the relevant principle(s) and explained according to that framework. Some doctrinal analysis may be based on the idea that the law is underpinned (or should be) by a particular moral or political philosophy and therefore needs to be analysed in light of its closeness to the ideal situation. In short, black letter lawyers seek to systematise and rationalise the law.

Doctrinal analysis uses particular techniques to render the law internally consistent (that is, is there is a thread of precedent into which this judgment fits?) or externally consistent (does this statute align with that statute, or does it align with the relevant principles?) As you will be aware from your earlier studies, the key ways black letter lawyers carry out their research agenda are by the techniques of deductive reasoning (sometimes called syllogistic reasoning) and arguments by analogy.

Using a black letter approach does not mean that your work should be confined solely to an exposition and clarification of the law. Critique and suggestions for reform of the law are entirely possible (and are expected at doctoral level) but they should take place within the premises of doctrinal analysis. A doctrinally-based thesis therefore, would not argue that the law needs reform because it is inconsistent with wider social values or is unfair to a sector of society, but because it is vague, or is inconsistent, and thus leads to uncertainty in its application.

Be aware also that black letter analysis is not a value-free form of methodology. Even though it may present itself as objective and unconcerned with the world outside law, black letter analysis is driven by values of coherence, certainty, and the idea that law can be made (if it is not already) ordered and stable, rather than a shifting mass of indeterminate rules with no connecting principles.

Jurisprudential Perspectives

Jurisprudential perspectives are a clear departure from traditional black letter methods of thinking about law. In this section we do not address traditional jurisprudential arguments about the nature of law itself; instead we present some theories about the way that law is developed and applied in society.

However, if you are going to write a jurisprudential thesis, you will of course need to have a solid grounding in the major schools of jurisprudence.

Legal Realism

Legal realism (not to be confused with Scandinavian legal realism) emerged in 1930s America as a reaction to the then dominant legal formalism movement or doctrinal analysis. The legal realism school argued that the outcome of legal disputes was not determined by considerations such as the consistent and logical application of the law, devoid of moral or policy considerations, but by other, sometimes non-legal, concerns. As one of its most famous proponents, the US Supreme Court justice Oliver Wendell Holmes put it:

> [T]he life of the law has not been logic, it has been experience. The felt necessities of the time, the prevalent moral and political theories, intuitions of public policy, avowed or unconscious, even the prejudices judges share with their fellow men, have had a great deal more to do than the syllogism in determining the rules by which men should be governed.

Legal realists worked to uncover the reality behind judicial decisions arguing that judges responded more to facts than to rules. While they were not prescriptive in their analysis, seeking rather to explain the law, legal realists did believe that judges needed to be aware of the consequences of a decision on society. They later expanded their analysis of law to take in the activities of other actors in the legal system such as civil servants. Legal realism suffered a considerable setback after the Second World War with the rise of the human rights movement, which put its faith in the rule of law over the legislature, and the critique of the legal philosopher HLA Hart, but it paved the way for other perspectives such as critical legal studies and the law and economics movement.

Critical Legal Studies

The critical legal studies movement began in the US in the 1970s. Drawing inspiration from Marx and later Foucault, CLS, as it is usually known, has as its central tenet the idea that law is a mask for the expression of power, and from that, the idea that law itself is not neutral, but an ideologically-driven form of power that serves the interests of the elite of society. CLS scholars, like legal realists, also argue that law is indeterminate, that is, it is not doctrine or precedent that drives the outcome of judicial decisions, but other factors.

CLS introduced the technique of 'trashing' to legal analysis, that is, the exposure of the hidden political nature of law, and the demystification of legal language to the same effect. CLS scholars are also concerned with the concept of 'reification', especially in the context of rights, where a concept acquires a form independent of and beyond its creation in a social context. CLS believes that placing one's trust in the legal system to protect rights is misplaced because of their potential for manipulation.

In this next section, we discuss three theoretical perspectives that can be grouped together under the general heading of 'jurisprudences of difference'. Feminist, race, and queer theories of law share with CLS the view that law is an expression of elite power but re-focuses that insight to marginalised groups in society rather than 'society' as a whole. Difference scholars have typically argued that the 'society' referred to by CLS scholars is inaccurately monolithic (and generally male, white, and heterosexual) and needs breaking down to expose the different experiences of particular groups.

Feminist Legal Theory

Feminist legal theory places women's experiences at the heart of legal analysis. It is relevant to those areas of law that traditionally affect women more than men such as sexual violence, sex discrimination, prostitution, pornography and reproductive rights but it can be applied to any area of law. Feminist legal theorists have also written in contract, torts, public international law, tax, and indigenous rights, to give only a small indication of the areas feminist analysis can touch. Of particular concern to feminist legal theorists are the concepts of gender, equality, dominance and power and how these are expressed and understood by law and through legal practice.

There is however, no one theory that can be called 'feminist legal theory'. In fact, feminist legal theory is simply an umbrella term for a variety of perspectives that can be found in feminism itself. These schools of feminist thought include liberal feminism, Black feminism, lesbian feminism, cultural feminism, Marxist feminism, radical feminism and postmodernist feminism.

Feminist legal analysis employs some distinctive methods, especially the use of narrative or 'story-telling' to ensure women's voices are heard, and 'asking the woman question': exposing those areas of the law that exclude or oppress women (Bartlett 1990). Feminist legal theory has come under attack by queer and critical race theorists both for its heterosexist and predominantly white perspective, leading to the development of the concept of 'intersectionality' to describe oppressions that have more than one axis.

Critical Race Theory

Critical race theory emerged in 1970s America as the gains of the civil rights movements began to slow down and even be chipped away. It also reacted to the civil rights movement's embrace of the liberal legal agenda, questioning the relationship between law, power, race and oppression, to develop a theory of law as a tool of racial oppression rather than the liberator the civil rights movement perceived it to be. Critical race theorists argue that racism is commonplace in the law and its application, rather than a deviation from the norm of 'colour-blindness', and in fact, that that very colour-blindness can be a shield for racism. Like feminist legal theory, critical race scholars consider narrative and story-telling important methodological tools.

Critical race theory initially focussed on African-American experience of the law, but has since developed Asian-American and Latino-crit jurisprudences as the experience of race and identity have been further deconstructed.

Queer Theory

Moving beyond the gendered critique of feminist legal theory and the binary hetero- or homosexual framework of earlier theorists, queer theory addresses issues of sexuality, transexuality and intersexuality within a legal framework. Amongst other themes, it investigates how the law responds to non-heterosexuals, the legal construction of gender and sexuality, and in particular laws relating to discrimination and marriage or partnership.

Postmodernist Theories of Law

Postmodernist theories of law represent the latest challenge to the doctrinal approach. According to postmodernists, law is not logical, nor ordered, nor coherent, as black letter lawyers would assume. The postmodernist project is the deconstruction of society's legal structures, its concepts, and the language of law itself, rejecting grand theories of law to reveal the disorder and diversity that lies underneath. Postmodernists also challenge the concept of objectivity, focussing instead on our subjective experience of law. In doing so, they raise questions about the universal applicability of law.

Law and Economics

Just as much a perspective as a technique, the law and economics movement, sometimes known as the economic analysis of law, can be traced back to the legal realists in its focus on non-legal considerations to explain and analyse the law. In brief, this method applies the tools of economic analysis to law with a focus on the free market's aims of economic efficiency and wealth and/or utility maximisation (it being said that the law simply reflects the economic system within which it is situated). Law and economics analysis can also be employed to explain the behaviour of actors in the legal system, showing why judges arrive at certain decisions, or why legislators pursue and create particular statutes. Some aspects of law and economics have been criticised, particularly the assumption of rational human behaviour (the study of behavioural economics being at the front of this challenge) and the focus away from justice and rights. Nonetheless, it remains a very influential school of legal thought.

Socio-Legal Research

Many different approaches and perspectives on legal research come under the socio-legal umbrella, but in essence, as the name implies, socio-legal research situates laws and legal analysis in a social (some would say societal) context. In contrast with black letter analysis, the socio-legal approach looks beyond legal doctrine to understand law as a social phenomenon or type of social experience. Socio-legal scholars often characterise their approach as the difference between 'law in books' and 'law in action'. Socio-legal research was first carried out in the criminal justice field, but these days it is being conducted in all areas of law. Socio-legal research can uncover and expose the (previously unquestioned) political nature of laws, show whether laws have achieved their intended effect, assist in law reform proposals by linking law and policy goals, and reveal how law actually operates in practice by shedding light on the experiences of different groups who come into contact with the law.

Olwen combined both traditional library research and empirical fieldwork for her thesis' methodology: 'The library research helped me understand the state of the law as it operates in domestic and international contexts. I used my findings to formulate the second stage of my research: I undertook a socio-legal ethnography using qualitative techniques. My field research aimed to learn from children how they understand law and legal structures and to see whether this is mirrored in the way that law understands and perceives children.'

By its nature, socio-legal research is inter-disciplinary, drawing on the tools and insights of disciplines such as sociology, social policy, anthropology, criminology, gender studies, ethics, economics and politics to explain and critique law and legal practices. Socio-legal research may also be theoretical, attempting to provide a social theory of law, asking what role does law play in society, or examining law as a form of power or a social system or a cultural practice. If you plan to undertake socio-legal research, make sure that you have a good grounding in any other discipline you intend to employ, either its methodological techniques (which we outline below) or its theoretical underpinnings.

Empirical Research Methods

Empirical legal research is closely related to the socio-legal approach to law. The term empirical means 'grounded in observation, experience, experiment or investigation'. While the methods of empirical legal research are many, what ties them together is their focus on the practicalities of law rather than its doctrines. Empiricists want to know about how the law works; what impact a legal change might have; how the actors in the legal system behave; if (and/or how) laws are enforced; how legal services are delivered; and how people are affected by and experience the law. In short, empiricists are interested in 'law in the real world', that is, law outside the immediate world of cases and statutes. Empirical research methods in law employ both qualitative and quantitative forms of analysis, and may include:

— Interviews
— Observations, for example, of courtroom interactions or lawyer-client exchanges
— Surveys (face-to-face or electronic)
— Case studies
— Data collection (of primary or secondary materials)
— Economic analyses
— Examinations of court records and transcripts

Parminder's methodological approach involved her using two rounds of interviews where she applied the insights from the first set to help her determine her research path: 'For the pilot study, I used unstructured interviews in two stages. This was because I wanted to take a wide-ranging approach that would enable me to incorporate the concerns of mental health professionals into the next stage of my research. I used "grounded theory" methods which involved drawing from the first set of interviews with community gatekeepers to decide who should be interviewed next and what the questions should be. Using this approach, I was able to remedy gaps in my own knowledge which I could not have gleaned using traditional doctrinal methods. This approach also created a supportive network of contacts when I encountered tricky questions later on. I plan to return to these interviewees to share the results of my project. In this way, I hope to give something back to the community.'

If you want to carry out empirical work, you will need to think about whether you have sufficient training to do the kind of research you are hoping to do. Consider whether you need training in how to construct and conduct interviews (including the rules on informed consent and compliance with data protection laws) or specialist courses in statistical analysis programmes and how to interpret the results.

James was an inexperienced researcher who nonetheless wanted to engage in some empirical work as part of his PhD. He was often exasperated by the difference between the law he studied in libraries and the experiences of law in practice that he saw reported in the media. He decided to devise an empirical research project based on interviews with those working in the industry whose regulation he was studying. However, James' research methods left a little to be desired and his supervisor was equally inexperienced and didn't foresee the problems. James found that his interviewees were reluctant to discuss some of the issues he believed were important and found that they were put off by his (unintentional) interrogatory style. He would have been better off first ensuring that he had adequate training to carry out empirical work and then engaging in a small pilot study before conducting the main part of his empirical work. Lesson learned!

A growing number of doctoral researchers are seeking to engage in empirical work. In some respects this is understandable (fieldwork can be exciting) and commendable (it can give rise to wonderful new insights). However, it comes with a health warning. Empirical research tends to take longer and can be a more risky venture. It can also be expensive—especially if there is a lot of travel involved. Before you commit to such a project consider carefully whether or not you have the time and funding to carry out the project.

Comparative Legal Analysis

Undertaking research on a comparative law basis is quite a shift from the usual national jurisdictional focus of most legal studies. Comparative legal research can open your mind to new ways of finding solutions to legal problems and requires you to confront any assumptions (often unconscious) you may be holding about how legal systems should operate. Comparative legal analysis might be undertaken within the same legal family such as common law jurisdictions or civil law jurisdictions, or between legal families—comparing customary systems of law to the common law, or comparing the common law to the civil law.

Comparative legal analysis is usually conducted for one of two purposes: either looking outside one's own jurisdiction to see how legal problems have been solved elsewhere—such as whether the New Zealand Bill of Rights would serve as a good model for Australia, or looking across jurisdictions or families of law for common threads of development or patterns in legal responses to societal issues—such as how do western European nations respond to the wearing of the burqa by Muslim women? These are referred to in comparative law discussions as the transplant approach and the harmonisation approach.

Comparative law scholars themselves disagree over whether comparative law can be said to have a distinct methodology outside the basic approach of comparing and contrasting. Unlike doctrinal analysis which focuses on rules and texts, or socio-legal methodology which looks to social theories and actions outside pure law, comparative legal analysis can be undertaken doctrinally or by reference to a particular social phenomenon you are hoping to find a solution to.

If you intend to conduct your doctoral research on a comparative basis, you need to make sure you are well-equipped to do so. Comparative legal research requires you to have a good understanding of the social, political and cultural context in which the relevant laws were made and now operate, so that you can feel confident in your analysis of the materials. You need to be able to conduct a balanced study in your chosen system(s), not one that deals with your national jurisdiction or system(s) in depth and the comparator only briefly.

And if your comparative investigations are not confined to the common law, then also consider carefully whether you have sufficient (legal) language skills to conduct research in more than one language. If you are going to rely on the translations of others, be careful that any doctrinal analysis does not rely too much on someone else's interpretation of the relevant materials.

In addition, ask yourself what value there is in making the comparison in the first place. Are you going to start from the premise that the systems you are going to compare are sufficiently similar (or from the same legal family) so that the approaches can be easily applied from one jurisdiction to another? Or will you be taking the view that a society with very different history and culture from your 'home' jurisdiction can nonetheless face a similar social problem and come up with a workable legal solution that might be of value to your own?

CHOOSING THE MOST APPROPRIATE METHODOLOGY

Deciding which methodology is most suited to your research will depend on the nature of your research project. In some cases it may be immediately obvious. If you are writing your thesis on the impact of rape-shield laws on conviction rates then an empirical approach combined with a feminist perspective may be a clear choice. But if you are doing research into the legal framework of stem cell research, then you may need to do some preliminary research into the most suitable methodology for your project.

One useful way of starting this enterprise is to look at the leading texts and articles in your chosen field. What sort of approach(es) do they employ? Is a particular methodology or perspective more or less dominant? Is there only one methodology in evidence? Think about the implications this has for your research: does this mean that there is only one appropriate way of conducting research in this area, or is the field calling out for a fresh new way of thinking about the topic?

You should also be able to approach your supervisor for advice about methodologies. However, be aware that your supervisor may be wedded to a certain perspective, which could lead to a difficult supervisory relationship should you choose to look at things differently, or your supervisor may feel unqualified to supervise work carried out according to methods they are unfamiliar with. Ideally, this is something you should have worked through in the preparatory stages.

Think also about the subject matter of your research project and your goals. What exactly is the argument you hope to make in your thesis? Do you believe that the law of contractual mistake has taken a wrong turn ever since a particular judgment? Do you want to know what factors influence juries in defamation cases? Do you think that insolvency law is being developed without proper regard to the interests of small creditors? By working backwards from your intended purpose, the most appropriate methodology should suggest itself to you.

DEVELOPING THE RESEARCH PROJECT

Depending on your chosen methodology, it might be appropriate to have a chapter or section in your thesis explaining why you chose a particular methodology and what your methodological processes were. Or you may want to set out the perspective you have filtered your research through, explaining its premises and identifying the key authors in the field. Doing so will help readers of your thesis make sense of your work and its arguments.

A methodology section should discuss the limitations of your chosen framework or approach as well as its strengths and suitability for your research—this shows that you have fully appreciated the nature and boundaries of the methodology. A methodology section is probably also the appropriate place for a discussion of the relevant literature relating to your methodology, although of course, you should also incoporate this literature into your analysis as you write your thesis. The extent to which you do this will depend on the selected methodology. If you're unsure how to cover the initial discussion of methodology and literature, be guided by your supervisor as to the conventions that apply to your particular doctoral programme.

How you use your chosen methodology within your research project is going to depend a great deal on the combination of that methodology with the subject matter of your research. What is important is not to treat methodology in isolation; even if you have a separate methodology section in your thesis, you should not treat it as something to be severed from the rest of your work—it should be incorporated into your analysis and writing as an integral part of your thesis.

If you are unfamiliar with the range of research methodologies out there, you may need to do a fair bit of preliminary research and possibly training beforehand so that you can make an informed choice. Once you feel confident in your decision, then you need to start planning how to integrate the methodology into your work.

The methodology itself may require you to do a lot of preliminary work before you can embark on your research. This is especially so if your research involves fieldwork of some sort. You may need to draw up interview questions, obtain ethics approval (more on this process in the next chapter), conduct the interviews and then collate the results before you actually have any material that you can work with.

If you choose a more theoretical approach where, say, you are planning to apply queer theory to different countries' laws on civil partnerships for same-sex couples, then your preparatory work may mostly involve familiarising yourself with the theoretical literature. You will need to be aware of your chosen theory's major premises, its debates and controversies, and its particular ways of understanding and critiquing the law before you engage with the law itself.

Other approaches, especially doctrinal analysis, will be more likely to see you delve early on into a slew of case law, statutes, and other legal materials—if primary legal sources provide both the subject matter of your research and your methodological framework, then it makes sense to tackle them both together.

CONCLUSION

Choosing the best methodology for your thesis is a decision you need to make in the early stages of your PhD. There is no 'wrong' or 'right' methodology, simpy the one that best fits with your research questions and interests. Questions to ask yourself include:

— Will I adopt a self-contained or applied approach to my legal research?
— Is my approach theoretical, practical or a combination?
— What methodology is best suited to the subject of my research?

Make sure that you understand how the needs of your methodology will affect the course of your studies, and equip yourself with the appropriate doctrinal or theoretical knowledge and any empirical methods training you might need.

4

Researching an Original Thesis

In the previous chapter we discussed some of the methodologies used by law doctoral researchers. Your methodological approach may change during the course of your research degree and in particular in the first year. Similarly, researching an original thesis is an evolutionary process—the thesis you submit at the end of three or four years may be very different from the one you thought you would write. That's to be expected of course: if you knew exactly what to write on day one, there would be very little point in conducting the research! This chapter considers the process of producing your thesis and examines the following topics:

— the research and writing process
— developing an original contribution to knowledge
— ethical issues in legal research
— research aids

Once you have concluded the chapter you should have a better understanding of *how* you can conduct structured and effective legal research. We discuss the process of devising an original research project, the cyclical nature of research and the difficult subject of research ethics. The final part of the chapter lists and briefly discusses some useful research aids that you may use during your doctorate.

THE RESEARCH AND WRITING PROCESS

Traditionally, the PhD in law involved library-based research in which the candidate produced a book-like thesis of anywhere between 60,000 and 200,000 words. The researcher would live an almost monastic lifestyle, reading and writing in the library and having the supervisor as the principal—and perhaps only—point of contact with the academic world. After years of toil, the candidate would emerge from this cocoon as a fully-formed academic ready to venture into academic life, researching and teaching. Or so the story goes!

Today, the research environment is much different, and although many researchers still operate as individual scholars pursuing their projects, the PhD programme is more structured and hopefully less lonely. In many institutions PhD researchers are now integrated into the faculty and—along with postdoctoral researchers—are part of the law school's community. In some, still rare situations, the PhD researcher may be part of a research team carrying out a larger project. You are now likely to have a series of training seminars, methodology and research skills classes at school or college level, and involvement in staff research activities.

The research process has also evolved. As we explored in the previous chapter, there are now a variety of methodologies employed by legal researchers to address questions posed by the law. While all research will begin in the library, for an increasing number of candidates it does not end there, but may instead involve interviews, observations or the collection and analysis of quantitative data. Even if your research remains largely library-based, your doctoral programme will not—with more opportunities to travel to conferences or to spend time as a visiting researcher at partner institutions or public and private sector bodies. These developments combine to produce a research experience that is far away from isolated ivory tower scholarship. However, in the end it's still down to you, the PhD candidate, to carry out the research and produce the thesis. In the vast majority of cases, the doctoral candidate selects the topic themselves and then refines it with assistance from their supervision team. It is the candidate who must carry out the research, analyse the data and, ultimately, write the thesis.

What does the research and writing process actually entail? It is likely that you will start off with a hypothesis: that police stop and search powers are used discriminatorily against ethnic minorities; or that principles of environmental protection have been mis-applied by the courts; or that the regulation of public space discriminates against counter-culture. Your task as a researcher is to devise a plan that will allow you to test that hypothesis and then to execute the plan. We have already examined research methodologies in chapter three. However, it is worth reminding ourselves that most research hypotheses can be approached from multiple angles. Thus, the examination of environmental principles could be examined either by (a) reviewing the case law of different courts and analysing the application of those principles or (b) conducting interviews with experts in civil society groups and even the courts themselves. These methodologies are equally valid but have different assumptions and may lead to different research outcomes. It is important therefore to make your methodological choices *consciously* rather than by accident, to explain the choices in the thesis and to be prepared to defend them in the viva. Your ideas on all aspects of your thesis will evolve during the course of your degree and you will revisit some of the earlier chapters a number of times. This is not a flaw in your research; it simply reflects the cyclical nature of research.

DEVELOPING AN ORIGINAL THESIS

The spark that ignited your interest in a particular topic is only the starting point towards developing your thesis argument. Remember the general benchmark for a PhD in law: the thesis must make an original contribution to knowledge. This requirement (along with the length) is what distinguishes a PhD from other writing projects you might have engaged in in university—you are expected to go beyond the boundaries of existing knowledge and understanding and offer something new. Achieving this is something of a mix between an art and a science. Remember, Edison famously remarked that genius is 'one per cent inspiration, ninety-nine per cent perspiration'. Of course, on the days when you're working hard and that one per cent can seem elusive, it's natural to wonder whether the perspiration is worth it. But if you have a methodical approach to your work you can increase your chances of making a breakthrough. And don't forget—you're only looking for an original contribution to knowledge—the genius can wait for later! Here we describe different stages in the research process. While we have laid them out in a particular order, each researcher's journey will follow a different path and you may find yourself jumping from one stage of the cycle to another—or even being at different stages in different parts of your research at the same time.

Situating Your Study in the Literature

While law doctoral researchers are often more likely to fall into the other trap (to read and read without writing), it's important to ensure that you do engage with the literature in your field before you try to make an original contribution. After all, you need to know what exists before you can offer something novel. This doesn't mean that you have to read everything written on your chosen topic before you pick up your pen and paper. As we outlined above, the research and writing process is a cycle and the process of situating your study in the literature is an evolutionary one. However, it does have to begin somewhere.

Identifying where your research fits in the literature is not a straightforward task. At the beginning you may be unsure on your position regarding key debates or you may find several authors equally compelling. Remember, your task is not necessarily to take sides and help to 'win' an academic argument; rather it is to critically engage with the literature in the field. To begin, it can be helpful to identify a handful of key authors on the topic and sketch out their thoughts. If your supervisor is a leading figure in the field, their work is a good place to start. It can be helpful to map out—on a single sheet of paper or the electronic equivalent—the scope of the academic debate on your subject. A graphic plot of the development of ideas can help you better understand how the literature has evolved and may help you see more easily where it is likely to go next. There are a number of research aids to help you with this form of 'mapping'—we will return to them at the end of this chapter.

In other disciplines, literature reviews tend to be quite systematic and are carried out in accordance with particular set methods. You can emulate this rigour in law. First, construct a search string—such as 'rule of law' AND 'terrorism'—which you will use in several different legal databases (see the final section of this chapter for information on useful legal databases). Second, identify those databases most likely to archive the literature you are trying to access. Adapt the string for the idiosyncrasies of the different databases and run the search in each one. Third, arrange the results into categories noting the number of results from each database. Possible categories could include the words used in the search string, the jurisdiction, whether any particular method was employed, the period of time covered, and so on. Fourth, review the abstracts (or titles or introductions if there are no abstracts) and identify the relevant literature. Fifth, read that literature in a systematic manner (perhaps chronologically, or by impact, according to the number of citations it has received) and make your notes. Having read some of the literature you may spot new terms to use in another search.

The process known as 'footnote surfing' or 'footnote mining' can also be a very fruitful one. As you read the articles you have identified, inevitably you will come across references to other works in the footnotes. Make a note of these and track them down once you have finished the first one. When reading those follow-up articles, again you will find references to other words—these again can be collected and their footnotes 'mined' for useful references. Eventually you will reach the point at which there are no new works appearing in the footnotes, and you keep seeing the same authors or articles again and again. At that point you can stop. It's important not to be overwhelmed by the sheer volume of possible works to follow up in the early stages of this process. But, since you cannot read everything at once, it's best to take a systematic approach: create a file of references, perhaps by date, or one of the categories you used in your database search, and simply store them away for later checking. It's also a good use of your time to start with the most recent article last as it will likely have the most up-to-date collection of references.

Just as law may borrow from social science methods, so too does it borrow from arts and humanities. Just as useful as the day in which you work methodically through a literature search is the day when you begin with one author and chain-read. Take a leading article on your research subject. When you've finished, look for a reference near the part of the article which most interested or inspired you, find that book or journal article and read it. Continue with this process for a few articles and you'll quickly find that your reading has moved very far from where you've started (and perhaps very far from your thesis topic). A good researcher will use a mix of the systematic and the serendipitous to ensure that she covers the literature on her subject while still being open to new and exciting ideas.

Identifying the Gaps in Knowledge

Having identified the key authors and the key debates, it is useful now to re-examine your hypothesis. Have other authors addressed it, and if so, how? In what ways do you believe their answers are insufficient? The idea of graphically mapping the debate and where your ideas fit into it can be help-ful once more at this stage. By identifying the gaps in the existing literature you will best place yourself to make an original contribution to the field. Even the most well-researched of subjects will have questions which remain unanswered, or have answers which need to be revised in light of recent developments. It is up to you to identify the niche into which you fit and develop your thesis accordingly. It is often this task—to be novel—that most worries doctoral researchers.

Being Novel

Making an 'original contribution to knowledge' can seem a daunting task at times. One relatively straightforward means of being novel is to analyse new problems posed by recent legal developments. However, recent developments may still be in flux and may therefore be difficult to research while in the process of change. Another means of being novel is to challenge the exist-ing academic debate. Perhaps the debate is polarised between two schools of thought which you believe have more in common than is believed. Or perhaps you suspect that existing research is based on assumptions that can be proven false. Some of the most impressive research takes an idea from one field and applies it to another. There are, in fact, many different ways to achieve origi-nality. In their book, *How to Get a PhD: A Handbook for Students and their Supervisors*, Phillips and Pugh list 15 different means by which a doctoral research project can be original (Phillips and Pugh 2010). Those which have greatest relevance to legal research include:

Developing a new methodological technique;
Testing another's idea in an original way;
Carrying out new empirical research;
Synthesising different work or using cross-disciplinary methods;
Carrying out research in a new jurisdiction;
Examining a previously unexplored research area;
Developing a new interpretation based on existing data.

Being original should not be difficult for a bright and dedicated doctoral researcher. In the early stages of the doctorate it is important not to become too concerned about originality but instead to develop the research project in accordance with good research practice. The originality will follow. Of course, some students do manage to research and write a lengthy doctoral thesis which fails the central test of making an original contribution to knowledge. However, if both the student and the supervisor play their parts correctly then this disappointing outcome should be averted. Even if a thesis appears to be tending in this direction it can be salvaged through the addition of critical work. A correct degree of self-critique at each stage of the research process will help to ensure that your work is challenging and original. It is also an important part of being a good researcher and will ensure that you are better equipped to deal with critique from others.

Identifying the Central Concept

Many legal research projects will involve more than one key concept. You may investigate how national security legislation affects human rights protection in a jurisdiction. What is the central subject: national security legislation? human rights law? or is it the academic debate relating to the two? Identifying the central subject of the research is one of the key challenges for doctoral researchers in the first year of their degree. In some cases it can take even longer. It is for this reason that it is not unusual for a doctoral researcher to produce a large volume of writing in the first months of the degree that will not form part of the submitted thesis. This can be both depressing and uplifting. It is somewhat depressing as it means that much of the soul-searching and hand-wringing you do in your first year is merely preparatory work. However, it is also uplifting because you can carry out this work safe in the knowledge that the difficulties you encounter are part of the normal process of evolving your research project and have been experienced by many researchers before you. As your central concept or concepts become clearer you will revise the work you've already completed and adjust your plans for future research.

Writing

Writing is not just the outcome of the research project, it is also an important part of the research process. Some researchers can carry out their research, analyse the data and then write up at the end. However, many researchers find that ideas evolve in the writing—the process of putting an argument down on paper can cause that argument to grow and evolve.

Don't be dismayed if you find yourself unimpressed by your early writing efforts, or if you supervisor considers these early efforts to be 'preliminary'.

It is not unusual to spend much of the first year of a law doctorate researching a broad range of materials and writing literature reviews and exploratory papers which will not, in the end, form part of your thesis. Remember, to stand on the shoulders of giants you first need to climb on top of them! Don't worry too much if you find yourself deleting large tracts of your early writing (or any writing) from your thesis—you may find alternative uses for this work. You may end up using the text in a published volume based on your PhD as doctoral theses tend to expect more of the reader than a monograph based on the thesis can. Or you may be able to publish some of your unused work independently of the thesis. Often the preliminary work that is carried out as background is done because no-one has done so already.

Peter was working on a particular area of human rights law. His project sought to analyse the implications of particular legislation for certain human rights. To his surprise he found very few articles that simply discussed the nature of the rights in question and the manner in which they had been developed by the courts in his jurisdiction. He wrote an 8,000 word exposition of the case law to help him better understand the jurisprudence on his chosen rights. While he ended up including only a short summary of this work, the effort was not wasted. A few months after submitting his thesis he updated the survey, deepened the analysis and published the resulting paper in a peer-reviewed journal. A year later it remained the most popular piece of work he had accomplished as it was the only comprehensive catalogue of the law in that area.

The type of writing you engage in will change during the term of your research project. The exploratory writing you engage in at the start of the project may be speculative but also quite ambitious. In the middle of your research project you are likely to engage in more descriptive writing as you record your methodology or data or conduct basic legal analysis of appropriate measures. Finally, towards the end of your project the writing will again become somewhat ambitious as you seek to come to some conclusions based on your research. Through this process you will find your 'voice' as a writer and hopefully the quality of the writing will improve as well. We return to the topic of good legal writing in chapter seven when we consider the writing-up process.

Discussing Your Work

It is important to air your ideas and let them develop through discussion. This can take many forms, the most obvious is discussion with your supervisor and other PhD students in your department. However you should also take the opportunity to present your work at appropriate conferences and seminars. There are now several annual conferences specifically aimed at doctoral researchers—we discuss these further in chapter ten. Use as many different fora as you can to discuss your work. Always take notes when asked a question or when someone is giving you feedback on your work—don't just rely on your memory. After discussing your work you can start the cycle all over again: thinking about new literature that has been brought to your attention, considering once more your central concepts, reflecting on your work and writing up your new thoughts. Your thesis should not be a will-o-the-wisp blown here and there by others' thoughts. But taking those thoughts into consideration will help you to develop a more robust argument and better defend your thesis in future discussion.

Martine found that talking to others about her work enriched her research: 'I have always been honest in talking about some of the gaps in my research and most of the time I have had great feedback. I have met a lot of people working in the field who rely on certain assumptions. By sharing my concerns about those assumptions I have found that people start reflecting on some of the questions and then give me suggestions about literature to investigate or in turn ask me questions that drive my thinking forward.'

Resting and Reflecting

Resting and reflection is a key part of the research process. When drawing up your time plan for your research project you should build in time to rest and reflect at every stage. Resting is important and you need to pace your research work over the course of the degree—a PhD is very much a long distance effort, not a sprint. Reflection allows you the opportunity to identify the strengths and weaknesses of your research to date while giving you the mental space in which to prepare for the next stage of research. Try to spend some time *not* working on your PhD but engaged in other activities—whether work or leisure. The time taken to reflect will not just help you to recover from the intensity of reading and writing at a high academic level but will also help your ideas to develop. PhD researchers have their ideas in the most unusual circumstances: at the cinema, in the shower or on the bus. Sometimes ideas come more easily when you are not trying to reach for them. It can be helpful to have paper and pen (or some electronic alternative) with you to capture these ideas. Don't overdo it though, you do need time away from your work, whether it's at the theatre, on the beach or in the park.

ETHICAL ISSUES IN LEGAL RESEARCH

It is increasingly important that the prospective PhD candidate is aware of the ethical considerations to be taken into account when conducting research. Today, universities require all research that involves human subjects to be approved by a research ethics committee before fieldwork is commenced. Obtaining ethics approval is a relatively new consideration for legal research. For those carrying out traditional, library-based research, ethics approval is unlikely to be needed. However, many law PhDs now have adopted social science research methodologies, where research includes interaction with human subjects. Such research requires ethical approval before it can be carried out. It's worth remembering that 'research into human subjects' covers a wide range of approaches—do not think that an interview with someone you know well (such as a former employer) or a single interview as opposed to a mass qualitative survey will necessarily be exempt from the need to gain ethics approval. Always check the relevant regulations first.

Research ethics can be a sore point for researchers. Filling out forms explaining precisely what is to be carried out, on whom, and what is expected to be learned may seem like a pointless bureaucratic exercise. For some lawyers it may seem irrelevant and for others like a check on their intellectual curiosity. It's certainly a long way from the romanticised idea of the researcher working in their laboratory experimenting with this and that and suddenly discovering something new. However, research ethics have been a part of academic inquiry for many years now—law is just playing catch up.

In the 1980s, two Australian scientists proved decades of scientific understanding to be incorrect when they established that stomach ulcers are caused by a bacteria called *Helicobacter Pylori*. Barry James Marshall and John Robin Warren were convinced their hypothesis was correct, but were prevented from testing it on humans (other than themselves) due to the ethics rules governing medical research. Marshall pushed the boundaries of knowledge by drinking a beaker of the bacteria and thus proving that it caused gastritis. Marshall and Warren later won the Nobel Prize for Medicine for their efforts. This tale might be misread as an indication of why ethics 'gets in the way' of good research. But it's important to remember that Marshall and Warren's unorthodox experiment *obeyed* ethics rules. While they were prevented from testing the hypothesis on other human subjects, they were not prevented from testing it on themselves. Thankfully, we can't think of any PhD in law that would require you to swallow the contents of a petri-dish! But many may require you to work with human subjects, in which case it's vital to follow best practice.

The Economic and Social Research Council, which funds, amongst other things, law doctoral research, describes six principles for ethical research in the social sciences:

— Research should be designed, reviewed and undertaken to ensure integrity and quality.
— Research staff and subjects must be informed fully about the purpose, methods and intended possible uses of the research, what their participation in the research entails and what risks, if any, are involved.

— The confidentiality of information supplied by research subjects and the anonymity of respondents must be respected.
— Research participants must participate in a voluntary way, free from any coercion.
— Harm to research participants must be avoided.
— The independence of research must be clear, and any conflicts of interest or partiality must be explicit.

It is these principles that the ethics committee or panel will have in mind when considering your application. The process of obtaining ethics approval can be an onerous one, but it's worth it in the end. Research ethics exist to protect you, your institution and the subjects of your research. Your institution's insurance will most probably only cover your research if you have obtained ethical approval in advance.

The Process of Obtaining Approval

One of the most frustrating aspects of obtaining ethics approval is the need to make reasonably firm decisions on the methodological approach to the research subject. The other side of this coin is that if you decide your research will involve human subjects you will be forced to grapple with the difficult methodological questions much earlier in your research project—an imposition that should help you to avoid the procrastination that can sometimes afflict doctoral research. It is important to contact the appropriate office as early as possible in the research process. The research ethics office at your institution will explain what you need to do to obtain approval and may help you to compose your application. If assistance is not forthcoming from that office, speak to your supervisor and programme director who will be best placed to give you guidance.

The principal determinant of how difficult it will be to obtain research ethics approval is whether the subjects you're studying are classified as 'high' or 'low' risk. High risk subjects include those who may be in a 'whistle-blowing' position in an organisation (such as judges or those working in certain civil service positions), vulnerable groups such as children, those in care, or those in state custody, or those who may disclose their own illegal activity. Studies that may subject participants to particular psychological stresses may also be high risk. A low risk study is defined, simply enough, as one that is not high risk. A high risk study is likely to be more closely scrutinised by an ethics committee than a low risk study.

You will be required to submit a sample of the consent form to be used with your research subjects which will specify the purpose of the research, the manner in which participants are involved, and how the participant may withdraw from the study if they have second thoughts. You should be able to obtain a sample consent form from your research ethics office or programme director and may be able to seek assistance from other researchers in your department in drafting it. Keep all the completed forms in a safe place as these are your proof that you have made the research subjects aware of your work before carrying it out.

Difficult Research Subjects

While there are several different triggers that can make a study 'high risk', most of those should not be relevant for law. As we mentioned above, it seems unlikely that law doctoral researchers will be conducting invasive medical procedures. Nonetheless, there are several other means by which a law study may become 'high risk' and it is worth considering at the beginning of your study whether your work will involve such subjects. If so, you will need to worth hard to ensure that you meet your ethics committee's requirements to obtain approval.

Illegal Behaviour

Given the nature of the subject, it is not unusual for doctoral researchers in law to examine illegal behaviour. However, such research will inevitably prove challenging from an ethical point of view. What would you do if a subject admitted committing a criminal offence? Or if they admitted to planning a criminal offence? If your work involves observations, you might inadvertently find yourself present during criminal activity. These are questions you will need to answer in order to obtain ethical approval.

Louisa was carrying out research into the self-regulation carried out by groups that committed minor offences. In interviewing these offenders, she would become aware of offences that may be committed or may already have been committed. If this was the case, Louisa would be under an obligation to report these offences to the police. However, the ethics committee helped Louisa frame her research in such a manner that both protected her from liability and prevented her from compromising the validity of the research. While it was a difficult process, by working with her ethics committee Louisa was able to complete valuable research in a difficult field.

Vulnerable Subjects

Vulnerable subjects may include victims of crime, in particular dangerous crimes such as assault or sexual offences. Studies that focus on witnesses in criminal investigations, in particular children, may also be classified as involving vulnerable subjects. Working with such research subjects will immediately render the project high risk and you will need to take steps to ensure that you protect those involved in your study from harm. Your ethics committee should be able to give you appropriate guidance in these circumstances. If you are dealing with vulnerable subjects you should also be aware of the need to protect yourself. Interviewing those who have experienced traumatic events can be harrowing. You must be as mindful of your own health and well-being as you are of theirs and remember that a certain degree of detachment is necessary for you to do your job appropriately. Do avail yourself of any training that is available to you to best equip yourself to deal with your research subjects—especially if they fall into a high risk category.

Failing to Get Ethical Approval

Remember: failure to obtain ethical approval in advance of research can have a significant detrimental effect on your research. You may have to exclude data obtained without approval from your study. Some journals will require evidence of ethics approval before accepting articles for publication. Therefore, while it may seem like a chore, especially for low risk research, obtaining ethics approval is a necessary and valuable stage in the research process. If your project is methodologically sound and does not present any major ethical problems then you will be approved—though not always at the first attempt. It is not unusual for an ethics panel to request that certain minor changes be made to the methodology—be it the means of data collection and storage or the method of obtaining subject consent—before finally signing off on a project. It is nonetheless worth considering what you might do if you fail to get research approval. Is your project contingent on the empirical research or could you alter your methodology and still produce an interesting and original thesis? While you will be disappointed, don't despair. Arrange to meet with your supervisor to discuss your options and perhaps you will be able to devise another, equally valuable, research project on the same topic.

RESEARCH AIDS

The more central the empirical component of your research the more you will need to think in advance about the appropriate methodology, supervisor, and—as discussed below—research aids and analysis tools. Whatever your methodology there are many research aids available to make the process of conducting your doctoral work easier. If you have picked up this book then you've already found one research aid. In this section we examine a range of useful research aids but you should be aware that these are not the only ones available to you.

Legal Research Databases

Whatever the subject of your research, you will begin, as discussed above, with a literature review. Today it is possible to search a wide range of legal sources using different databases of primary and secondary materials. For literature, the three most useful databases will be Westlaw, LexisNexis and HeinOnline. The Index to Legal Periodicals (ILP), Index to Foreign Legal Periodicals (IFLP) and JSTOR are also useful—the latter is particularly helpful for historical work. Each database offers access to a different range of sources and this may also vary based on your own institution's subscriptions. Access to these databases is usually obtained through an 'Athens' or 'Shibboleth' system—one password that will give you access to all of your institution's electronic journal subscriptions.

The Social Science Research Network (ssrn.com) may also be of use. SSRN is used by researchers across the world to upload working papers and even articles that have been published (subject to copyright constraints). Often, you may find research available on SSRN that is at the forefront of the academic debate and this can help you keep on top of the research being conducted in your area. Your library may offer training on how to use these resources and if so, it can be very worthwhile to take that training quite early in your degree.

Equipment

It is worth identifying at the outset what equipment you may need and enquiring as to its availability in your institution. All researchers require the same basic equipment, while those doing fieldwork or other forms of empirical research may require more specialised equipment. The basics are, of course, a computer, printer and internet connection. Thanks to the wide range of electronic journals available, it is now probably possible to complete a PhD with just these resources. However, most students will also be heavily reliant on a good law library. This is the basic equipment and should be provided by your university. However, for anyone engaging in research beyond the library-based, other equipment will also be necessary.

Fieldwork Equipment

Different forms of fieldwork will require different types of equipment. Probably the most typical fieldwork carried out by empirical researchers in law is the interview. Interviews will require recording equipment such as a Dictaphone, mp3 recorder or other device. If you do conduct interviews, and regardless of your methodological approach, you are likely to want to transcribe the recordings—which can be a lengthy and tedious process. As such, it may be worth investigating if your institution offers transcription services. Finally, you may need qualitative data analysis software. Again, this is something you should discuss with your programme co-ordinator. If you need to purchase any equipment for your research, it may be worth discussing the availability of funding with your programme co-ordinator or funding body. It may be that your institution will purchase the equipment and allow you to use it, but regard it as the institution's property to be made available to all researchers.

Analysis Tools

Those who conduct empirical research will require the use of software to help analyse the research data. The availability of that software is a factor you may wish to take into account when choosing the appropriate venue for your doctoral research. A department which has several researchers (either doctoral researchers or members of the faculty) who engage in empirical research is more likely to have the appropriate tools for data analysis than one that does not. If your own department is not au fait with the requirements of empirical researchers then be sure to bring it to their attention. You may also be able to rely on resources in other departments within your institution—a school of social science should be well-equipped in this regard.

Research Assistance

It is rare for a doctoral candidate to engage a research assistant. As many doctoral candidates are at the beginning of their academic career, it is much more likely that they will be employed as a research assistant for an established academic. Furthermore, the doctoral thesis is expected to make an original contribution to knowledge that is solely your own work (generally you will sign a statement attesting to this upon submission of the thesis). However, there are certain circumstances—health problems for example—where assistance may be permissible. You may need to employ a typist if you have difficulty using a computer. It is not unusual for those writing in their second language to solicit the assistance of a native language proof-reader.

Lane was a typical over-worked doctoral candidate who also held down a full-time academic position while carrying out his research. He developed certain repetitive strain injuries as a result of excess stress on his body while in the final months of writing-up. Having struggled on for weeks, Lane finally discussed the matter with his supervisor. The supervisor arranged to have a research assistant type up Lane's hand-written corrections, allowing Lane to complete his research on time without doing any further damage to his health.

Current Awareness

Current awareness is the name given to resources that keep you up to date on the latest legal developments in your field. Sources of current awareness include ordinary news outlets, specialist magazines and journals, and, increasingly, online news aggregators, blogs and twitter feeds. Keeping abreast of the latest news in your area is an essential part of producing a novel thesis.

Social Networking Tools

While Facebook (www.facebook.com) remains the most well-known and most popular online social network, it is not necessarily the most useful for academic networking. The difficulty in managing your personal data, as well as the near-impossibility of separating academic links from holiday photos, makes Facebook something of an unwieldy tool for the researcher. In recent years some more focussed alternatives have evolved, including, most notably, Academia.edu (www.academia.edu). This site is based on the same principles as Facebook but is explicitly aimed at helping you 'follow the latest research in your field'. Its network varies from discipline to discipline and even within research fields so you may wish to explore whether or not there is a network of researchers in your field on the site.

Twitter (www.twitter.com) is growing in usefulness as a networking and research tool. Twitter limits users to sharing short messages of 140 characters. There are many famous Twitter users such as Stephen Fry and Britney Spears who use the system to share the minutiae of their day with the world. However, Twitter is also used by leading intellectuals and researchers to highlight news stories, academic articles and random websites that have come to their attention. By subscribing to the messages of some academics in your field you can find out what they find interesting on a day-to-day basis. Some fields are better served by twitterers than others, but it's worth searching for a few key authors in yours to see if they tweet.

Blawgs

You will almost certainly have heard of blogs (a neologism derived from 'web logs') which serve as simple websites that have become one of the most popular online publishing tools in recent years. B*lawg*s are blogs about law. There are a wide range of excellent blawgs available to read for free—and many provide not just current awareness, but also analysis of recent cases and legislation. To properly harness the power of blawgs, it can be useful to sign up to one of the many free aggregators. Aggregators take the blog's output, usually called an RSS feed (RSS: really simple syndication), and use it to display the blog's content on another website. The genius of aggregators is that they allow you to read all of your blogs in one place. Popular online aggregators include Google Reader and Bloglines, while offline aggregators (which download the blog's content to your computer) include RSSReader and FeedDemon. We've collected a list of law related blogs in Appendix C, but remember that online resources are constantly evolving so some of these may be extinct when you go looking for them, while it is likely that others will have sprung up. Start off with one or two useful blawgs and you'll soon get the hang of it. If you like what you see, you might even start your own blog to help you build a public profile and disseminate your research findings. New blogs are emerging all the time so do spend an hour or two 'aimlessly' browsing the web and see where your travels take you.

Research Diary

It can be extremely useful to keep a diary of your research process. Most institutions will now require you to fill out periodic progress reports and naturally a research diary can make this reporting process easier. Some institutions will use a Gantt Chart, named after the engineer Henry Gantt, which is a detailed form of bar chart used to plan and review the progress of a research project.

Doctoral research in the arts and humanities often does not lend itself to the precise planning that a Gantt Chart requires. Some tools which are useful in other disciplines such as the health and natural sciences are not appropriate for law. Whatever your own institution's requirements, it is certainly worthwhile to keep track of your progress. A diary is particularly useful as it serves several functions: a log of your thoughts each day, an easy way to see just how much work you've completed in a week and what you've spent most of your time on, and a great way of reminding yourself about important tasks and deadlines. There are many ways of doing this—both electronic and non-electronic—but one of the most useful is a large day-to-view desktop diary. Find whatever works for you and use it—you'll be grateful when you're trying to remember where you found a particular article 18 months after you first read it!

Human Resources

You should never forget the most obvious resource—your peers, supervisor and other colleagues inside and outside of your department. At the outset of your research project you should get to know the different people in the department with responsibilities in relation to the doctoral programme. Your supervisor is always your first resort, but the departmental tutor or programme director should also be willing to answer emails, there will be administrative and library staff who can help with your research, and other academic staff who will be willing to discuss your ideas. People are always your most valuable resources—their support will help you through the difficult times and their knowledge of the department and of university life will assist you in countless little ways throughout your degree.

CONCLUSION

The aim of this chapter was to introduce you to the research and writing process and to explain some of the most important aspects of that process. The key points to remember are noted below.

— You do not have to reinvent the wheel during your PhD and you certainly don't have to do so in the first year. Allow yourself to develop as a researcher and the project will develop too.
— If you are conducting research that involves human subjects you *must* obtain ethical approval. Investigate the process of doing so early in your research project and you won't be caught out by your institution's requirements.
— There is a wide range of research aids available and your institution should provide training in how to use them. Taking advantage of these opportunities in the first year of your project can save you days worth of time later on.

Your first port of call on all of these matters is likely to be your supervisor—and your relationship with your supervisor is the most crucial one in terms of a successful PhD. The next chapter addresses this most important of topics.

5

Supervision

This chapter deals with what may well be the most important relationship of your academic career. Although you are ultimately responsible for your success in the degree, your supervisor can have a considerable impact on your doctoral experience and sometimes beyond it. The most fortunate doctoral researchers find themselves developing a long and lasting relationship with their supervisor. The right supervisor can smooth your progress through the PhD, continue to inspire you after you move on, and act as a mentor for the rest of your career in academia or elsewhere. The wrong supervisor can derail your studies and leave you feeling confused and directionless. Most supervisors, being generally decent types but human all the same, fall somewhere in the middle.

It is important to think about supervision and supervisors well in advance of choosing your institution. Once you have chosen your institution and begun your research under your supervisor there is still much to be negotiated. You don't want to start off with unrealistic expectations that later have to be corrected, or fail to put in place procedures that could have made your research life much easier had you adopted them from the beginning. Earlier we discussed the process of finding out about and approaching different potential supervisors. Here we consider some of the aspects of a successful supervisor-student relationship.

In this chapter we look at the following topics:

— The supervisory relationship
— Making the best of your supervisor
— Supervision problems

THE SUPERVISORY RELATIONSHIP

No two supervisory relationships will be the same but it can be helpful to talk to some current or former students of your prospective supervisor before you make your final decision. This chapter will give you an idea of the sorts of questions you should ask to see if your supervisor is the right fit for you.

The supervisory relationship will change over time. As you progress through your doctoral programme, it is very likely (and in fact expected), that the relationship with your supervisor will evolve into more of a collegial one, where you take on more and more the role of an expert engaging in a dialogue about your research and its directions with a fellow researcher.

Learning how to negotiate your supervisory relationship is good training for future professional relationships. You may work more closely with your supervisor than with any other academic for quite some time (perhaps until you have research students of your own to supervise). If you can make the supervisory relationship work then you may well be cut out to navigate the sometimes difficult world of academic departmental politics.

How Many Supervisors?

Throughout this book we've referred to supervisors in the singular. The traditional idea of research supervisor focussed on a single supervisor acting as mentor to your research. However, it is becoming more common to assign two supervisors to each student: one will be the primary (or principal) supervisor, and the other the secondary. Typically, most (or all) of the supervisory responsibilities will be allocated to the primary supervisor. What then, does the secondary supervisor do?

In some cases the two supervisors will act as co-supervisors and play an equal part in guiding you through your research degree. This might be the case if your work is interdisciplinary or involves the use of a research methodology with which your primary supervisory is unfamiliar. In others the secondary supervisor will simply act as a back-up, to step in if the primary supervisor is unavailable, for example, by going on sabbatical, or in some cases, as an overseer of the work of a less experienced supervisor. The nature of your relationship with each of them is something you should ascertain at an early stage, though you should be open to those relationships evolving as your research does.

Formal Requirements

Unless you have completed a Masters degree by research, you are probably unsure of what exactly to expect from your supervisor. Where can you start looking to find out? Each university should have a formal document of some sort (probably entitled 'Code of Practice for Postgraduate Research Degrees' or something similar) that sets out the minimum requirements and expectations for supervisors at your institution. There may also be a specific Code of Practice for each department. This is a very useful document. You can supplement your own university's document with the QAA's (the Quality Assurance Agency for Higher Education, a body which carries out audit functions in relation to tertiary education institutions) Code of Practice which has a section on supervision within postgraduate research degrees.

The Code of Practice should tell you generally what your supervisor's responsibilities are towards you as a student, including providing guidance as to the frequency of meetings, the monitoring of your progress (and any formal progress reports that need to be made) and giving feedback, the provision of information about skills training and teaching during the degree, as well as advice on publications and the eventual submission of the thesis. Institutional requirements aside, the key responsibility of supervisors is to guide you through the process of writing an extended piece of original research. How this is done may take many forms.

The Development of Your Research

As a minimum, supervisors should make themselves reasonably available to discuss your (written) work or ideas and give you feedback on your work. At the beginning of your degree, you will probably rely more heavily on your supervisor for guidance. You will have already submitted a research proposal as part of the application process but your supervisor may well ask you to refine it, do further research, or consider new angles. Your supervisor may also suggest putting aside your research proposal and spending some time instead reading widely in your area before coming back to the proposal with fresh eyes and a deeper knowledge of the area. This sort of experience can be frustrating, especially if you feel you have already put together the perfect proposal and want to get down to work. However, you should try to view this as a learning exercise, part of the process of becoming a fully-fledged independent researcher—and take the opportunity to benefit from your supervisor's experience as a researcher.

Your supervisor should also be able to help with identifying and securing training in any research methodology necessary to your research plans. We have discussed researcher training in chapter four. Don't be afraid to look around your institution for appropriate training and then discuss it with your supervisor. Supervisors are busy people and they may not be aware of everything going on in your university. A good supervisor will be pleased that you have taken the initiative to seek out appropriate courses. Be sure to consult with your supervisor before actually embarking on any programmes though.

As you progress through the degree, you should work out with your supervisor how the process of submitting your work and receiving feedback is going to be managed. There are of course as many different ways of operating as there are supervisors and students. We make some suggestions here, but you should feel free to adapt or devise your own way of working through this process.

The first method requires you to be very organised and have a clear idea of what you are hoping to achieve with your thesis right from the start. Under this system, after submitting a research plan, the student works methodically through each chapter or chapter section in an agreed order (you may for example, wish to do a research methodology chapter first, or you may want to set out the basis for your thesis with an extended case study of the situation that sparked the decision to enrol for a doctorate). Before the writing commences, the student sends the supervisor a chapter outline for discussion, setting out what the goals of the chapter are, the major and minor headings, and a description of how this chapter relates to other chapters in the thesis. Once supervisor and student are happy with the plans for the chapter, the student can begin the writing of the chapter. The chapter (hopefully in nearly final form) is submitted, and a meeting for feedback is then scheduled. The student then makes any adjustments to the thesis as required. The process is then repeated until the thesis is completed.

Another way of working is a more thematic approach where you schedule general meetings with your supervisor, not to discuss specific chapters, but to talk about your ideas and how you hope to fit them into your thesis. These don't need to be at regular intervals and your written work may be very much in draft form or incomplete when you approach your supervisor for comment. You may go through several versions of a chapter, going backwards and forwards with your supervisor, before you feel a chapter is done.

It may be that you begin with the more thematic approach before proceeding to the more methodical chapter-by-chapter approach once you have determined the precise scope of the research project. Or, you may begin methodically but need to think thematically at key moments as the focus of your research evolves.

A good supervisor (and a good doctoral researcher) should be willing to be flexible as to the approach taken to supervision. If one method isn't working then try another. It is helpful to know what you want to achieve from each meeting—regardless of your approach to supervision.

Professor Smith had a research supervisee who seemed to be forever planning. Each meeting would consist of the researcher explaining how a new book, article, or conference presentation had prompted a rethink of the previous thesis design. The student would arrive with a whole new plan worked out but with no writing done. In the end Professor Smith had no choice but to insist that the student sit down and write a thesis chapter before returning for a further meeting. He set a date a month in the future and told the student to submit a draft chapter by that date. The student did, they met and discussed the work and the student began work in earnest. Professor Smith's student was simply afraid to commit to a plan—by insisting that the student write, he was forcing the student to stop their serial (and temporary) infatuations with the work of others and to find their own project.

Whatever form your supervision takes, it is important to write and receive feedback on your writing throughout the degree. In some institutions students are required to write papers on their broad area of research during the early months. Though these may not form part of the submitted thesis it is nonetheless a good idea to get into the practice of writing and discussing your written work with your supervisor. You don't want to find out too late in your degree that your supervisor's approach to feedback on writing is unsuited to your needs. Getting into good writing habits early on will prepare you and your supervisor for the years that follow.

Progress Monitoring

Supervisors are also responsible for monitoring your progress through the stages of the degree. While once universities were content to allow students to meander through their degrees, sometimes over a decade or more, universities are now under pressure to make sure that doctoral students complete their studies within four years of enrolment for full-time students or the equivalent for part-time students. This has had an impact on the way in which your progress is monitored and any problems addressed.

This responsibility for timely completion is usually discharged through formal university reporting requirements and may take the form of an annual, bi-annual or quarterly report setting out what you have done since enrolment or the last report in terms of thesis progression. For instance, you may be required to specify how many chapters you have written, what methodology training have you had, reports on any fieldwork or other empirical research you have done. The university may also require you to report on other academic activities such as conference attendances or presentations, and any publications. The supervisor will usually be asked to make some comment on your continued enrolment and the likelihood that you will finish within the expected timescale. You may also have some input into these forms so make sure you keep a good record of your activities since the last report was filed. If any problems with your progress are flagged as a result, then you will probably be referred for a progress meeting with the person in your department with overall responsibility for PhD students to discuss how you are going to overcome these and how the department can help. Even if your university does not have formal monitoring processes, you should ensure that *someone* is monitoring the progress of your research project. This will most usually be your supervisor but it can also be helpful to occasionally engage a fresh pair of eyes to the project—perhaps a second supervisor or another academic with experience in your area.

Your supervisor will have pastoral responsibility for you and should make you aware at the beginning of your studies of the support services available to you at your university. It's important to discuss any problems you are facing (we discuss some of the most common of these in the next chapter) with your supervisor so that action can be taken to help you. Honesty is the key ingredient in the supervisor-student relationship. You need to be truthful about your expectations, capabilities and, as the degree progresses, about what you have achieved and what you can realistically achieve. Equally your supervisor should be honest about what their expectations are and what they can offer as supervisor. They should give you frank feedback about your work and your likelihood of success. If you can both manage to be honest in your dealings with each other then the relationship is likely to be a happy and fruitful one. Don't forget the need for flexibility—meetings will occasionally be rescheduled and sometimes your supervisor will miss a deadline (just like you). You need to understand the demands on your supervisor's time as much as you expect them to understand the demands on yours. While a pattern of missed appointments might give cause for concern, the occasional rain check is to be expected.

Transfer from MPhil to PhD Registration

If your university has structured the doctoral programme in this way, an important milestone in your progress will be the transfer from MPhil to PhD status. This is usually a formal event which takes place after the first or second year of enrolment (that is, nine to 18 months in real time) to assess whether your work is meeting doctoral standards and whether you have made sufficient progress in the doctoral programme to be allowed to continue.

Each university's requirements will differ, but generally you will have to submit a substantial piece of work (such as two chapters or the equivalent), an outline of what you intend to achieve with the rest of the thesis, and a timeline for doing so. Check whether your department has a file of previous transfer submissions that you can have access to—these can be a valuable guide as to the standard and level of detail required for a successful transfer. Make sure that you are familiar with the regulations that apply at your university by studying them closely.

As well as the documentation, there may also be a participation element to the transfer event. You may have to attend a 'mini-viva' where you defend your work before a panel of academics. An alternative is that you present your work at a seminar and answer questions about it. These sorts of events are very useful for providing you with feedback about your work from other academics and giving you a platform to talk about your research in front of a (usually) sympathetic audience. The perspective of academics who are coming fresh to your work can open up new ideas and possibilities for your research, so don't discount their views simply because they haven't been involved in your research from the beginning. While it is a different event, our chapter on the viva can give you some idea of what to expect and prepare for if you are required to present your work in some way.

The transfer event usually has four possible outcomes:

— Unconditional transfer to PhD status
— Conditional transfer to PhD status
— Remain in MPhil programme
— Deregistration

Obviously everyone aims for the first outcome but outcomes two and three are not the end of the world, even if they seem that way at the time. They represent an opportunity to reassess where your research is going and whether you are suited to PhD study. It is always better to have this moment in your studies earlier rather than later. Of course the research process is not the same for everyone and some researchers will have a more successful first year than others. However, if you do find that you struggle in the first year it's important to consider why.

It may be that the transfer problem identifies some structural or methodological issues with your research that need addressing. Or the transfer may have revealed that you have not fully thought through how different aspects of your work are going to come together into a coherent thesis. Work with your supervisor to come up with a plan for dealing with these issues and make sure that you re-submit your work (or face a further panel) within the time limit specified.

If you do get a recommendation that you should continue on as an MPhil student and not upgrade to PhD registration, then do not think that you have failed and abandon your studies completely. A Masters degree is a worthwhile qualification in its own right, representing hard work and intellectual rigour.

Participating in the Academic Community

In academic life, your reputation depends on the academic community's assessment of the merits of your scholarly output. With this in mind, supervisors should encourage you to enter onto the stage of the academic legal community by publishing your work (check to what extent this is permitted under your university's regulations and also whether there are any rules on joint publications with your supervisor), attending and presenting at conferences, and participating in other activities that help disseminate your ideas such as research symposiums or colloquia, or making submissions to parliamentary committees. Your supervisor may also head a centre or institution of some sort and may be able to give you a junior role in the centre's work which will help in raising your profile. As an established academic, your supervisor is probably part of a number of informal and formal networks of which hopefully you can be invited to become a member. Of course, while these opportunities are to be embraced, don't forget that the thesis must come first—make sure you schedule your activities well and don't be waylaid by the myriad of interesting activities going on at most universities. Sometimes supervisors forget what it is like to be starting out so don't be shy about reminding them that you may need an introduction to the academic community.

Personal(ity) Matters

The nature of your relationship with your supervisor is going to depend very much on the personalities of the people involved. Each relationship will be unique. Neither of you is going to be able to change who you are, so it is a good idea to think about how your personality affects the way you work. Equally important is who your supervisor is.

For example, are you the organised, methodical type who prefers to be left alone to get on with your work and who never misses a (self-imposed) deadline? Are you the type who works in short productive bursts and would rather only see your supervisor when you have something to discuss? Or perhaps you need a bit more prodding and supervisor-imposed structure because you tend to get very enthusiastically side-tracked by topics that are not strictly relevant to your research project?

Similarly, do you work in a linear way, working your way through each chapter in turn? Or do you like to work thematically, bringing everything together at the end? Do you need to do a lot of preparatory work such as training in a certain methodology or mastering a statistical analysis programme, before you can start your research, let alone the writing, or are you in a position to dive right in and begin writing the first chapter?

You should also think about whether you are a verbal or auditory learner: do you want to deal with your supervisor through your written work, submitting a chapter and receiving feedback via email or do you prefer to have an extended discussion of your ideas with minimum reference to your written work?

You should be able to expect your supervisor to be generally qualified in the field of your work, interested in your thesis project, to treat you and your ideas politely and with respect, to be an active supervisor, that is, to be accessible, to read your work and give you feedback, and to guide you through the doctoral and institutional maze.

How this translates into your unique supervisory experience depends of course, on the supervisor. You will find that some supervisors are very hands-off during the doctorate, happy to leave you to it, only stepping in when you ask for help, while others want to be involved in every aspect of your research from the very beginning. Some may take the view that the supervisory role is a purely professional one, to be kept strictly to the confines of the office, with the discussion never straying from thesis-related matters. Others will take a 'whole person' approach, providing a sounding board for all aspects of your life.

Think about how your two personalities combine: if you need structure and your supervisor is the hands-off type, you could soon find yourself in difficulties and not making much progress. If you want to focus on your work only and your supervisor wants to hear about your cat's latest ailments over a drink or two at the pub, then things could become quite uncomfortable.

If you have an irreconcilable personality clash with your supervisor, and you know that you will not be able to continue with that person, seek advice from the academic in charge of PhD programmes immediately. These things do happen and there should be processes in place to effect a change of supervisor with minimum fuss. Do not leave it until the situation is beyond repair: your research will suffer, and your reputation within the department will most likely too.

MAKING THE BEST OF YOUR SUPERVISOR

Even if your supervisor is the best supervisor in the history of doctoral supervision you will still need to do a little work to make sure you get the best out of your time together. In this section we discuss how to get the maximum benefit possible from the supervision process.

Meetings

How often should I meet my supervisor? This is a common question from students at the beginning of their degrees. The general pattern is that students and supervisors meet more frequently and regularly in the first year, with fewer meetings as you progress through your degree. The university code we mentioned earlier will probably spell out the minimum number of meetings you should expect to have. If it does not, you can ask the director of your programme for some guidance.

You and your supervisor should agree a schedule of meetings that reflect the stage of your degree and your expected progress. You should aim to meet at least once a semester, and more often in the early stages. However, some people prefer a more flexible approach, asking supervisors for meetings only when they have work they want to discuss. Most meetings are one-on-one, but some supervisors also like to have additional group meetings with all their supervisees together. These can be very useful fora for you to discuss your ideas in an informal environment with others in the same area, and gain motivation from (or commiserate with) others going through the same process.

Supervision Diaries

One useful suggestion is to keep a record or 'supervision diary' (paper or electronic) of all your meetings with your supervisor. In it, you can record not only the main points of the discussion of your work, but also any references or other work you need to pursue, as well as the next steps agreed upon. This record can help you keep track of your progress (for those occasions when you feel you are going nowhere, a written record can be a cheering reminder of how far you have come); it can also jog your memory to what you should be doing once the meeting is over as you can easily forget things afterwards if they are not recorded at the time. The supervision diary can stand alone or be integrated into the research diary mentioned in chapter four.

Feedback

Receiving constructive criticism of your work from an expert is one of the great benefits of being a doctoral student. The feedback you receive during your doctorate is probably going to be quite different from that in your earlier studies: you are unlikely to receive page-by-page comments of anything you submit; rather, you are more likely to find that your supervisor concentrates on an aspect of what you have done and asks you to re-think or re-write it. This does not mean (except in extreme cases) you have done something wrong; rather, it means that you might do things differently. In the end, your supervisor's suggestions are but that; they are not orders you must follow, for that would undermine the whole purpose of doing a piece of extended research.

Do not be dismayed if your supervisor does not wholeheartedly endorse everything you have done and do not take criticism personally. This is hard to do in a doctoral programme where you are invested in the uniqueness of what you are doing, but it is good preparation for academic life, where your ideas will be subject to (sometimes fierce) scrutiny. Look upon all critique as a learning exercise: being challenged to explain your ideas, your approach, or your choice of subject can be very useful in making you examine your choices.

Your Responsibilities

It may seem from what we have written so far that supervision is a one-way street where you simply enrol in the degree and are then 'supervised'. Not so! Supervision involves two people. That means you have a degree of responsibility for making things work too. While at this stage in your academic career you cannot lay claim to match your supervisor in terms of expertise and experience, there are things you can do to enhance the supervisory experience.

All supervisors have had experience of students who are their own worst enemies: they come to meetings with ill-thought out plans or ideas ('I thought I would talk to some people about that'; 'I want to look into Soviet-era show trial archives even though I don't know any Russian'); they ignore the supervisor's comments for improvement or further research; they turn in draft chapters late and unreasonably demand feedback according to their timetable ('I need this back within a week because I am going on holiday soon'); they have an excuse for missing every deadline set ('My dog died again'); they never develop any independence and are still too reliant on the supervisor ('I couldn't find a reference for that point; can you tell me what I should be citing?' 'Where do I find the Common Market Law Reports in the law library?'); they are full of enthusiasm that never translates into anything concrete; and they avoid attempts by the supervisor to set deadlines for them and don't respond to emails. Hopefully if you are reading this book then you are not one of those students.

Supervisors tend to warm to students who have enthusiasm for their topic and can turn it into written work; who have clear ideas about the progression of their research and how to achieve their goals; who come to supervisors for help promptly when they identify problems or stumbling blocks with their research; and who are open to suggestions for improvement and change. Students who work consistently on their project and continue to make progress with their work are also looked on favourably. And being punctual for meetings and proofreading your work before handing it may seem like small things, but they contribute significantly to making a favourable impression. Learn your supervisor's pet peeves (will submitting your draft in Helvetica see it consigned to the bottom of the in-tray?) and be sure to avoid them.

SUPERVISION PROBLEMS

In an ideal world, this section would not need to be written. Indeed, the majority of postgraduate research students rate the supervisory experience highly, as research from the Higher Education Academy shows.

Question	PRES 2007	PRES 2008		PRES 2009
	% Agree	% Agree	Mean	% Agree
I.a My supervisor/s have the skills and subject knowledge to adequately support my research	82.2	83.8	4.33	84.4
I.b My supervisor/s make a real effort to understand any difficulties I face	73.0	75.1	4.09	76.0
I.c I have been given good guidance in topic selection and refinement by my supervisor/s	68.4	72.3	3.98	73.0
I.d I have received good guidance in my literature search from my supervisors/s	62.1	64.0	3.78	64.8
I.e My supervisor/s provide helpful feedback on my progress	70.8	72.8	4.01	73.7
I.f My supervisor/s are available when I need them	71.7	74.0	4.05	74.7

Source: Table 4 in C Park *The Research Student Experience: Lessons from PRES* (The Higher Education Academy, 2009)

But don't forget, the student-supervisor relationship is inherently unbalanced in the supervisor's favour. Although you may end up with greater subject expertise than the supervisor, your supervisor retains the upper-hand in terms of institutional and personal authority, security within the department, and probably age as well. That imbalance brings with it the potential for exploitation. Supervision problems can take a variety of forms, from the personal to the professional.

If you do end up being unhappy with your supervisor, don't let the problem linger in the hope that it will somehow improve if you ignore it. It won't. It will be more likely to make things worse. You do not want to want to be in the position of considering legal action for your abandoned or failed PhD against the university: it will be stressful, it will most likely mean the end of your academic career before it has begun, and you are unlikely to win.

For many of the problems we identify below, there will be university or departmental codes governing the situation, and an identifiable individual or office to turn to in confidence for help resolving the problem. You can also turn to the Office of the Independent Adjudicator (the body responsible for dealing with student complaints against higher education institutions) for advice.

Poor Supervision

Some supervisors simply do not do a good job. They may not be interested in your work and so neglect it. Feedback may be delayed and minimal. Meetings may be hard to arrange and too brief when they do occur. Others may have been forced into being your supervisor as part of fulfilling some departmental administrative requirement and resent the time supervising you takes away from other more interesting and rewarding projects. Others may simply have too many responsibilities, especially if they fall into the category of academic celebrities mentioned in chapter two, and won't see your thesis as a priority.

Given the key role a supervisor plays in the success of your degree, act promptly if you find yourself in this situation. First, speak to the supervisor and try to have a reasoned discussion as to your requirements as a student. The supervisor may not be doing a good job—but might change if they are made aware of the problem. If the problem cannot be solved by speaking to your supervisor then see the person in your department responsible for PhD students and request a transfer to a more appropriate supervisor, or ask (if you know this is feasible) to arrange a swap between your primary and secondary supervisors.

Academic Exploitation

Most students want to please their supervisors. Unfortunately, some supervisors take advantage of this, relying on how flattered a student feels when the supervisor involves the student in his work. One particular problem arises in cases of co-publication where the supervisor takes credit for work done by the student. Equally, while it is both useful and enjoyable to occasionally offer a lecture or seminar on your supervisor's course, teaching is a time-consuming activity. If you are engaged to a significant extent in your supervisor's teaching you may need to consider the impact on your research—and whether you should be paid for your time.

Another problem occurs when students find themselves in the role of unpaid research assistant on the supervisor's own research projects, often to the detriment of their own work. In these sorts of cases, there is not very much you can do while you are in the middle of it. But be aware of any negative impact of being involved in your supervisor's work and limit your future availability in the politest way possible if you do think that you are becoming subsumed by your supervisor—you do, after all, need to make progress on your thesis and begin building your own profile.

Of course, not all co-publications are the result of academic exploitation and it is possible to have a good working relationship with your supervisor. Some students engage in mutually-beneficial collaborations with their supervisors, if not before the degree then certainly afterwards. The key, as ever, is honest communication about what you both expect from any such project.

Discrimination and Harassment

The student-supervisor relationship is founded on trust. You have to be able to rely on your supervisor to guide you through the stages of doctoral research with personal and professional integrity. Discrimination and harassment destroy that trust and represent a failure of the supervisor's integrity on both fronts. You do not have to put up with this sort of behaviour. Approach the relevant university student support services and the departmental person responsible for PhD students and request a change of supervisor immediately.

Sexual Relationships

While uncommon, it is not unimaginable that a sexual relationship might develop between supervisor and supervisee. Such a relationship is inherently dangerous as the supervisor is in a position of power over the supervisee and there is a great risk of exploitation. The supervisor may well be in breach of their duty of care to the student. Even if both the supervisor and student act in good faith there is an obvious risk that the relationship may sour and the research degree may be adversely affected. If you find yourself in such a relationship with your supervisor you should seek alternative supervision (or end the relationship). That way you can allow your personal life and your professional one to develop without one putting the other in jeopardy.

These are all worst-case scenarios. In most situations problems with your supervisor are likely to be more moderate. You may feel that you are not meeting with sufficient frequency—or perhaps you're meeting too often. Your supervisor's feedback may be too vague to let you know if your progress is satisfactory or not. Your supervisor may not be supportive of other activities you need to undertake to help build your career—from publishing to attending conferences and teaching. If any of these problems arise then you should simply discuss them with your supervisor—many of them can be easily solved.

CONCLUSION

Your supervisor may well end up being the best friend you make in academia. Before you get to that point you need to build a relationship of trust and respect. Treat your supervisor well and you can expect to be treated well in return. Remember that in supervisory relationships, as in many things, honesty really is the best policy.

If, despite your best efforts, or through no fault of your own, the supervisory relationship breaks down, or was never really working in the first place, don't be shy about seeking help and advice. The supervisory relationship is key to a happy and successful doctoral experience, so make sure that the one you have works for you.

6

PhD Problems

No university degree is easy and it seems fair to suggest that the degree of Doctor of Philosophy is the hardest of all. As such, while some students may sail through the process and move from research plan to graduation with barely a hiccup, the average doctoral student will find their path to completion has many twists and turns. In the previous chapter we examined the supervisor-supervisee relationship and the problems that may arise in that context. In this chapter we consider some of the other common problems experienced by doctoral researchers and consider how they can best be addressed. The problems examined here include:

— Someone else wrote my PhD!
— Boredom and lack of motivation
— Financial problems
— Writer's block
— Health problems

Even if you are fortunate enough not to experience the difficulties discussed here, it may be useful for you to be aware of them so that you can help those around you through the tough days. Many of these problems are not specific to law doctoral researchers and so friends and colleagues from other disciplines may also experience these problems.

SOMEONE ELSE WROTE MY PhD!

Your perennial fear as a doctoral research student will be that someone else will write and/or publish your thesis before you. This fear is natural, but not something worth losing too much sleep about. It is natural because the test for a thesis is that it makes an original contribution to knowledge. There may be an impact on your originality if someone else comes to the same conclusions as you using the same methodological process. Thus, reading the work of those writing in your area tends to become tinged more and more with excitement and trepidation as you proceed through the research degree. It is exciting as it means that you are not alone, there are others investigating the same research questions as yourself and you are part of that wider community. But it will also be a somewhat fearful process, wondering whether the next page will contain the idea that you thought of—or worse, the idea you wish you had thought of. Despite the thrills it provides, it is not worth worrying too much about someone else writing your PhD. No two research projects evolve in exactly the same manner and even projects that come to similar conclusions may use different sets of data or different methodologies. Thus, the rival research project that you thought 'wrote your PhD' may simply provide further evidence to corroborate the findings of your own work. Even if your research project is library-based and not based on original empirical research a skilled lawyer will always be able to find points of contrast between two works. Read any potential rival publications closely and you may find that there are nuances which, when examined, allow you to push the debate even further.

There are some steps that can be taken if you want to ward against ill fortune. First, a thoroughly researched literature review should make you aware of those who are working in your field. By following the publications of the key scholars you should be aware of the direction of academic debate and make your own contribution with your research. Second, keep an eye on databases of recently-awarded grants and current research projects. The Current Legal Research Topics database at the Institute of Advanced Legal Studies in London aims to compile the details of all MPhil and PhD research projects currently underway in the UK. While the database can only be as complete as the information submitted to it, it is certainly worth taking a look at (and of course contributing to) so you have some idea of what is being examined in your field. Third, network! Scholars working in your field may well have doctoral students of their own and you can get to know them through academic conferences and even by cold-call emailing. Most scholars welcome interest from those working in their area and it is likely that you can allay your fears over a cup of coffee and make a useful contact in the process.

Donna was in the middle of the second year of her doctoral research degree when she discovered that a thesis had been submitted at a neighbouring university with an almost identical title to her own project. Worried that she had spent a year and a half working hard on the topic only to be usurped even before she wrote-up, she took a trip to the university's library to check out the potential rival. Three hours and two cups of coffee later, Donna had satisfied herself that not only had the other, recently graduated doctoral student not written her thesis, but that she had managed to probe some of the questions in a deeper and more meaningful way. The rival thesis would provide a useful reference point on some areas of law without ever threatening the originality of her own contribution to the field.

As long as you keep these pointers in mind you'll have no need to worry—the only person who will write your PhD is you. It will be a unique contribution to the field from your perspective. As long as you work hard and stay engaged with the academic debate there should be little chance of someone stealing your thunder.

BOREDOM AND LACK OF MOTIVATION

We have pointed out at several points in this book that a doctoral research project is akin to a full-time job. It demands your complete focus and attention on a daily basis and while it involves some flights of intellectual fancy, there's also a whole lot of nose-to-the-grindstone work. Conducting a literature review can be a tedious and repetitive task. Days spent compiling and reviewing the case law on a particular topic can sometimes seem like a waste of time when the line of enquiry proves fruitless. It shouldn't come as a surprise then that from time to time you may become bored or frustrated with your research. Those feelings don't necessarily mean that academic life is not for you or that you are not capable of completing the doctorate. Rather, they are a predictable response to any work environment, even one as exciting as the furthering of knowledge. So when faced with boredom or a lack of motivation try not to despair but to diagnose the problem and treat it.

The first step on the road to treating boredom is to identify it. In chapter four we mentioned a research diary as a useful way to keep track of how your research is going. A well-kept diary should be able to provide the first indication that you have become less productive than usual. If you find that you're not getting much done, take a look at what you're trying to achieve in a working day and working week. Are you asking too much or too little of yourself? Break large tasks up into smaller ones and make a note of when you complete a task—regardless of how small. At times boredom or a loss of motivation is a product of feeling like no progress has been made. By demonstrating to yourself that you are in fact making progress you may regain your motivation. And even if completing small tasks doesn't suddenly revive your enthusiasm for the project you will at least be getting some work done.

Maintaining motivation is such an important part of the PhD process that we've heard of institutions running training for supervisors to teach them how to motivate students to motivate themselves. Being part of a cohort of students undertaking the degree together offers one of the best safeguards against falling motivation. While the research project in law is usually an individual effort, it is less isolating if it is one of several individual efforts being undertaken by a group of intelligent and motivated people. Meeting people outside of your own peer group can also help. If you're in the middle of a slump seek out a conference or seminar in your field and attend it. We discuss elsewhere the way in which a carefully-chosen conference may be a good opportunity for some professional networking and a chance to update your knowledge of the field. What's more, attendance at conferences and seminars can inspire you both in terms of ideas for your own research and also as to the value of that research itself. If there's no convenient conference to help lift you from the doldrums you can seek out staff or students working in your field with whom to discuss your research. Their enthusiasm will be infectious and may help you to recover yours.

A change of scene can also be useful. Depending on your work practices and your institution, you may spend the majority of your time in a library, working from home, or if you're lucky, working in an office as part of your law school. Whatever your working environment, altering your practices from time to time can keep your working life fresh and help stave off boredom and research stagnation. It is likely that there will come a time when your useful research routine needs to be broken to allow you to continue working productively. If you regularly work in your office consider decamping to the library for a fortnight and see if you are inspired by the learning around you and rediscover your researching zeal. On the other hand if you usually work in the library, why not consider another venue—it may be another library, a quiet (and sympathetic) café or even your living room if your accommodation arrangements permit it. You can also stave off workplace stagnation by building variety into your routine. To do so, spend at least one day a week working somewhere other than your regular office. If Friday is library day you may begin to look forward to it and the change of location may help jolt your brain back into action.

Roger was having difficulty focussing on his research—a combination of low motivation and plenty of distractions meant that he wasn't getting enough done each day. While he would start off the day with the best of intentions, the morning would slip away on low-level tasks like answering email and checking blogs and the afternoon would find him reading a few articles in an attempt to salvage something from the day. He realised that he had fallen into a bad work routine and decided a change of environment might help. After two weeks of working in a library he had analysed an area of law key to his thesis—helping to build his theoretical framework and producing an article that was published in a peer reviewed journal. The change of scene prompted increased productivity which itself increased motivation.

Don't be dismayed if you find your interest in your research waxes and wanes. It's natural to be less enthusiastic about a project from time to time. As with any of the problems discussed in this chapter first identify the problem and then address it. Achieving targets like completing a chapter, presenting a conference paper, or publishing an article will help to restore your confidence in your project and your ability to complete it.

FINANCIAL PROBLEMS

A doctoral research programme is a financially demanding undertaking. Tuition fees for the programme tend to be several thousands of pounds (and more if you are an international student) and you will require further funding to support yourself during your degree. We have already examined the question of how to fund doctoral research in chapter two. It is important to have a clear idea of how you will finance your studies from the outset of your degree. If you have not secured a scholarship for your fees and maintenance needs you will need to examine whether or not you can afford to embark upon the research programme. Even if you believe you have the financial resources to do so, it is worth considering how secure your financial position is and to take steps to safeguard against any change in your circumstances. However, even the best-laid plans can fall victim to circumstance and some doctoral researchers find themselves in the unfortunate position of losing their financial support during their degree.

As with any financial problem there are two means by which you can make ends meet: increase income or reduce expenditure. Either method can present difficulties for those undertaking a research degree programme. The most obvious means of increasing income is to take on part-time work (or to find a higher-paying part-time post if you are studying part-time). There is a range of activities that may both complement your research and help you increase your income—in particular by becoming employed either as a teacher in your institution or as a research assistant to an established academic. Some universities have a formal position which aims to train you to be a member of the academic community while you complete your PhD. If you cannot find career-related part-time work you may be able to find some other employment. We have met doctoral researchers working as part-time librarians, office assistants, caterers and even sports coaches. However, any such work carries with it a cost in terms of your time. Any time you spend on a part-time job is time you cannot spend on your thesis. If your part-time job is physically or mentally demanding or requires you to work unsociable hours then it may take even more time out of your schedule. The time cost may be less if the work is relevant to your research but you should be aware of any lost time. Some institutions provide hardship funding for students who encounter unexpected financial difficulties during the course of the degrees. Rules on these funds vary and they are unlikely to provide a sufficiently steady income to rely on the fund alone but they can be very useful as a stop-gap if you experience difficulty.

Margaret started her PhD studies as a full-time student in the hope that securing some scholarship funding would help her make ends meet. Unfortunately strong competition for all of the scholarship schemes to which she applied meant that she did not secure any extra funding. After discussing matters with her supervisor, she decided to switch from full- to part-time study and adjusted her timeline accordingly. In the second year of her PhD she secured work as a tutor in her college which allowed her to fund her part-time studies. The close proximity of her teaching to her research area meant she did not have to spend too long preparing each lesson and the teaching experience also helped towards securing other opportunities. Margaret is now on track to complete her PhD—precisely because she took appropriate steps and didn't just stick her head in the sand and hope for the best.

Decreasing expenditure can also be challenging. Apart from expenditure on accommodation, the single greatest item on your budget is likely to be your fees. As such, one means of addressing a financial shortfall that is relatively common among doctoral researchers is to move from full-time to part-time study. Being registered as a part-time rather than a full-time student usually involves paying half the fees for the degree and having twice as long in which to complete it. However, part-time study may itself come with hidden costs. If you lose your full-time student status you may lose the right to be exempt from local taxes, the right to discounted public transport and certain other financial benefits. Thus, you will need to calculate if the financial benefit gained from changing your registration status exceeds the financial cost entailed in doing so. Your institution's rules on changing registration status may not, in any event, permit you to switch to part-time for financial reasons. If this is the case you may have little choice but to interrupt your studies until you secure funding to continue your research. Whatever path you take to restoring balance to your budget, do make sure to check with your institution's support structures that you are making the right choice.

WRITER'S BLOCK

The difficulty of sitting down and writing a thesis of 100,000 words is not to be underestimated. In the course of undertaking that seemingly mammoth task there are bound to be times when the blinking cursor on your computer screen offers too great a challenge and you find yourself struggling to write. This feeling—referred to throughout the world of written composition as writer's block—is frustrating at best and demoralising at worst. Writer's block may be a symptom of lack of motivation, frustration at the quality of your work or a feeling of lack of inspiration. Whatever the cause, you can take action to try to break your block and get your thesis back on track.

Switching writing methods may help. Most of us now do almost all of our composition on a computer using word processing software. Sometimes it's the apparent formality of putting words on screen that deters us from writing. The sense that you should only write something into your Chapter 1. doc file if you know it's going to be perfect is understandable. However, the reality is that writing is an evolutionary process. The draft you write today will be redrafted tomorrow and edited and edited and edited. Therefore there's little point in being too precious about what you write. If you find yourself tending towards perfectionism when you write on-screen then switch to paper and pencil—it can be easily erased. Try sketching out your thoughts for the chapter or chapter section in question. You might start with some headings and sub-headings and then try a few sentences. You might find you break through your block and the words will flow more easily.

If you're finding it hard to motivate yourself to sit down and write a 10,000 word chapter then try breaking the writing up into shorter blocks. One of the benefits of researching the law is that there should always be something to write about. If you are having serious difficulty getting words on paper then why not choose a legal development relevant to the chapter you're researching and write a short analysis of it. Though you may not even include the work in the finished thesis the process of writing the analysis may help break through your writer's block. In an interview in 1971 the acclaimed writer Graham Greene discussed his writing method with the *New York Times*. He said:

> I hate sitting down to work. I'm plugging at a novel now which is not going easily. I've done about 65,000 words—there's still another 20,000 to go. I don't work for very long at a time—about an hour and a half. That's all I can manage. One may come back in the evening after a good dinner, one's had a good drink, one may add a few little bits and pieces. It gives one a sense of achievement. One's done more than one's thought. (*New York Times*, 12 September 1971)

Greene went on to say that when he began writing he set himself a target of 500 words a day. Despite this relatively modest target Greene wrote over 30 novels in his lifetime. When you sit down to write your thesis, remember that just a few hundred words a day can add up to a 100,000-word work over time. Instead of seeing the blinking cursor as a challenge, try to see it as an opportunity to add to your growing work. It just might be the first book of many in a long and successful career.

HEALTH PROBLEMS

We are legal researchers and not clinicians and so we hope we can be forgiven for our rough division of health problems into the physical and the psychological. While some PhD students will experience the former during the course of their degree, most if not all PhD students are likely to experience the latter. It is important to be aware of the potential impact of any health problems on your doctoral research. The common cold can prevent us from working for a week, more acute or more chronic illnesses can have an even more serious effect. When planning your research project it is useful to have some time built in for the unexpected—whether these are health problems or something else. If you have existing health problems at the start of your degree you need to decide how much you wish to disclose to your supervisor or the director of your programme. Making your institution aware of health problems will ensure you get the best possible help during the course of your degree. Nonetheless, it is understandable if you are reluctant to reveal personal matters to an institution or a member of staff you have just met. The degree of disclosure will require you to build up a level of trust and it is likely that this will take time. You may wish to make your supervisor aware that there is a health issue at the outset of your studies but wait until you feel more comfortable sharing the details to explain further.

Psychological problems may be related to the doctoral research process itself. Whether it is boredom and lack of motivation or something more serious like depression—you may well suffer from some psychological problems during the course of your PhD. Stress is perhaps the most likely affliction. Vitae describe common indicators of stress as follows:

— a 'churning' stomach, 'butterflies'
— difficulty in sleeping
— always feeling tired
— a racing heartbeat
— tightness across the chest
— depression, a feeling of hopelessness
— tearfulness

It's important to recognise when you are under stress and to take action to reduce it. Try to identify the causes of the stress—being over-worked, having poor time-management, not taking the time to relax or enjoy pastimes, or being in conflict with fellow students or staff. Once you've identified the cause you can talk to your fellow students, supervisor, friends and family about dealing with it. Stress management is an ongoing activity for most of us in our working lives but the nature of the doctoral research programme can cause you to have to deal with serious stress over several years. You can get off to a good start by thinking about how you manage your time and building your personal support team at the start of the degree so that when the pressure is on you are in the best possible position to deal with it.

Stress can often be linked with more serious problems such as depression. Depression is a much more common problem than might be popularly perceived, with Depression Alliance UK indicating that one in five adults in Britain will experience depression in their lifetime. Depression can manifest itself in mild, moderate or serious forms. Some symptoms of depression are feeling sad, bored, anxious, tired or fatigued, having irregular sleep patterns or having difficulty sleeping, a loss of interest in usual pleasures, unexplained aches or pains, or a loss of self-esteem. If you experience these symptoms over a prolonged period of time you may wish to consult with your university's counselling service or student welfare office. These services are typically offered on a confidential basis and so you can use them with confidence.

Will suffered from mild to serious depression throughout his doctoral research degree. Despite receiving a lot of support from his colleagues within the department his institution was not very helpful. While he eventually received some support he was left with little confidence in his ability to carry out a research degree. Despite having a strong background in research he was left feeling unable to cope and without the required emotional support to conclude a difficult degree.

Will's story is not unusual and there may well be a Will in your law department. Establishing student support groups and lobbying your institution for better support for mental and physical health can help students who don't even know they are facing a problem. Demand help—you're entitled to it!

Even if you don't experience any health problems during the course of your research it is a good idea to stay healthy. Recall the trite but true Latin maxim—*mens sana in corpora sano*—a healthy mind in a healthy body. Exercise causes the body to release endorphins which trigger feelings of happiness and well-being. While we cannot claim to have seen conclusive evidence, there is some (both scientific and anecdotal) that suggests aerobic exercise can also help brain function. So it may well be that a healthy researcher is a happy researcher and also a productive researcher.

CONCLUSION: GETTING HELP AND SOLVING PROBLEMS

You should always remember that, whatever the problems you face during your PhD, there are people who can help you. Your supervisor is likely to have had experience with a wide range of PhD problems and will often be your first port of call. Your friends inside the PhD programme and from other walks of life can provide support and sometimes solutions. Your institution should provide a range of student support services, from counselling to health services to financial advice. It can help to identify those who can assist you before you actually encounter any problems. Make yourself aware of the services available at your university at the outset of the degree and you will be well-placed to address any problems when they arise.

If you are unfortunate enough to encounter serious problems that may affect your research progress you may wish to investigate if you can interrupt your studies for a short period. Rules on interruption vary from institution to institution but you will typically be allowed to interrupt for a total period of one to two years during the course of your degree. If you are interrupted the clock will not be ticking on your registration period and you may not have to pay fees. Thus the interruption can be a useful way of taking some time out from your degree to address the problem you've encountered. When you have resolved the matter you can return to your research project and resume work. However, an interruption should not be requested lightly. If you are researching a developing area of law then time out from your degree may leave you with more work to do to catch up on developments. As such, you should discuss any interruption with your supervisor and the director of your programme before you make your final decision. The earlier you make your supervisor, friends and institution aware of a problem the more they can do to help.

It's not just your own problems that may affect your progress. If your spouse or partner becomes ill or you experience a bereavement then you need to be aware of the implications for your research. Good news can also have an effect on your research. A change in your life situation, whether it's marriage, the birth of a child, securing a new job (if you're a part-time student) or moving home can all take their toll. You need to consider the significance of any such life event for your research and adjust your timetable and expectations accordingly. As always, discussing the matter with your supervisor is a useful first step in working out how best to adjust to your new situation.

Finally, however hard it may be to believe when you are surrounded by professors, lecturers, postdocs and other doctoral researchers, remember that most people go through life happily and successfully *without* a PhD. Important as the degree may seem, it is not your life's work and nor should you want it to be. And there's little chance of you successfully completing it if you pull on blinkers and cease to become aware of problems with your health or wider happiness. Taking care of yourself is the best way to take care of your PhD. Some key points to remember are:

— *All* doctoral researchers experience one problem or another in the course of their research studies—so there's no shame in admitting to having difficulties.
— Just because you experience problems doesn't mean you can't complete and go on to have a successful academic career.
— The earlier you identify and share a problem with your peers and supervisor the faster you can solve it and get on with your work.

Whatever problems you face, remember that many doctoral researchers have faced them before and still successfully completed their degree. In the next chapter we consider the writing-up period—the stage of the research degree immediately before you submit your thesis.

7

Writing-up

There comes a point in the lifetime of every thesis where the author decides that enough is enough. The literature has been reviewed, the data collected and analysed, the thesis' hypothesis has been tested and some conclusions have been arrived at. If the thesis in question concerns legal research, it is likely that there will already have been much writing done. However, even when the researcher has been steadily compiling chapters over the course of three years, there will still come a point where they must decide that they are writing-up: consolidating all of the research and writing into a single document that will be the 'thesis'. This chapter addresses questions such as:

— How do you know when it's time to write-up?
— What does turning a collection of chapters into a thesis entail?
— What is good legal writing and how do you produce it?
— How should you go about producing the final draft?

While this chapter is likely to be most useful to you when you begin your writing-up period it does contain some useful advice to bear in mind throughout the PhD. Thus, even if you're not yet ready to enter the final stage of your degree you should read this chapter carefully to get an idea of what's ahead of you in a year or two. Some of the advice—in particular on good legal writing—will be useful throughout the research and writing process.

KNOWING WHEN TO WRITE-UP

The structure of the PhD degree varies from institution to institution. However, you are typically allowed between six and 18 months on 'writing-up status'. The nature of 'writing-up status' will also vary, but it may involve decreased student fees (or no fees at all) and an expectation that you will submit within a set period of time. Writing-up status is your institution's way of acknowledging that you are coming to the end of your degree, that you are (hopefully) no longer relying on the institution's resources to the same extent and therefore that you should not be paying the often hefty fees that full- or part-time students pay. Some institutions attempt to incentivise submission by requiring you to pay a writing-up fee and then refunding the fee if you submit by a certain deadline. You should ascertain your institution's rules on transferring to writing-up status early on in your degree so you know what the requirements are before you can move to this final status. In addition, you should discuss the writing-up period well in advance with your supervisor—they may have a particular mode of working with their writing-up students that you will want to be aware of. Your supervisor is also likely to know what your institution's attitude towards the writing-up period is and may be able to give you advice on institutional practice that you won't find in your student handbook. It is worth noting that not every student will require a writing-up period. If you submit within three years of ordinary full-time study or the equivalent period of part-time study then you may never be formally on 'writing-up status'. That doesn't mean that you won't go through the usual 'writing-up' stage of the doctoral research process—you'll just go through it earlier. The rest of this chapter will still be relevant to your work so read on.

The start of the writing-up period is a good time to start thinking about the examination process. Thus, you may wish to consider your institution's rules on the format and style of the thesis (discussed below), the selection of your examiners and any paperwork that must be completed for you to enter for examination. Knowing who your examiners are at this point will allow you to keep your key audience in mind as you write up your thesis. That's not to suggest that you will change your work simply to suit the examiner's point of view—but a good writer is always mindful of their audience. The task of choosing your examiners will fall to your supervisor. You will have two—one 'internal' and one 'external'. The internal examiner may be from another college within your institution (this is likely to be the case if you are studying in Cambridge, London, Oxford or a similar large university) or even from within your own faculty (although this is much more unusual). The external examiner will be another expert in your area of law but from further afield. Discuss the choice of examiners carefully with your supervisor to ensure you get the best possible panel for your thesis.

How you begin your writing-up period will in part be dependent on the nature of your doctoral research project. If you have been conducting library and archival research into the concept of limited liability for corporations and have not engaged in empirical research then much of your work to date will have focussed on reading and writing. As such, you are likely to have a large bulk of text already written and are therefore looking at a rewriting rather than a writing period. On the other hand if your research project has involved interviewing prisoners about their experience of the criminal justice system you may begin your writing-up period with significantly less writing done—as you will have spent much of your time 'in the field' conducting the interviews and in your library/office/coffee shop transcribing those interviews and analysing the data. It may seem unfair but those who conduct empirical research are likely to take longer to conclude the degree than those who do not. The other side of this coin is that those who do conduct empirical research may find it easier to find something new and exciting to say about the research topic—so each pathway has its pros and cons. Even if you have been conducting empirical research you are likely to have some of the written work already completed before transferring to writing-up status. Your ethical approval process should have required you to write a rigorous methodological chapter and you are also likely to have completed a literature review. Whatever your pathway, you will begin the writing-up period with some if not all chapters in draft form. The challenge that lies ahead is to turn these chapters into a coherent thesis.

TURNING A COLLECTION OF CHAPTERS INTO A THESIS

Most doctoral researchers in law still aim for the traditional 'big book' thesis. This means that having written anywhere between four and eight chapters (it can be more or less but most doctorates fall within this range) the task for the writing-up period is to arrange the existing work so that it presents a clear and compelling discussion of the research topic and advances a thesis which can be defended in the viva. That task will entail working on each of the chapters to ensure that the thesis as a whole introduces your hypothesis, explores it, develops an argument and concludes. Very few doctoral students will have produced a work of this length prior to commencing their research degree. Managing a large piece of writing is in itself a skill and one which the doctoral research process should help you develop. Hopefully the doctoral thesis and a monograph based on it will be the first but not the last significant publication of your career.

If you have not already done so, then the start of the writing-up period is when you should seek out your university's regulations on what a thesis should look like and get into the good practice of ensuring that your written work conforms to them. These rules may be as simple as stipulating a word limit or as complex as requiring a particular referencing style, specifying margins sizes, heading styles or appropriate fonts. Remember, the rules have probably been designed to ensure that the thesis is easy for the examiners to read and for you to refer to during the viva if necessary. Of course, there may be no such logic and the rules may simply be drawn up to comply with the collective eccentricities of your institution's examination board. Whatever the rules and however they may offend your aesthetic sensibilities make sure you comply with them fully. Theses can be refused for failure to comply with these requirements which, if it were to happen, would turn a happy submission day into a rather glum one. So if your institution wants the headings in Wingdings font then so be it (though in that case it would be rather unusual as *Taking Rights Seriously* would look like this: ✲☉&⒣■℔ ☼⒣℔≋◆✦ ◆⒨□⒣□◆✦●⊠⬧).

At the start of the writing-up period it is necessary to review the work completed to date and to plan your time until submission. Work out which chapters are more or less finished, which will need significant revision and which ones, if any, have not yet been written. You will generally need to revise each chapter to make it work as part of the whole—but this is particularly true of the introductory and concluding chapters. It can be a good idea to give over a certain (but limited) amount of time to these at the start of the writing-up process to allow you to get a sense of the whole thesis, but don't devote too much time to them at this stage as you will almost certainly need to revise them again before submission. The introduction and conclusion are re-examined below. While they are in some respects the most important parts of the thesis they should be easier to write when you have finished the remainder of the work.

The principal thesis chapters may take any one of countless different approaches to structure. If you have engaged in fieldwork and have collected and analysed a large volume of data then your thesis may be structured in a quasi-scientific fashion with an introduction, a literature review, a methodology chapter, an exposition of the data, a chapter analysing the data and a conclusion. However, few law theses take this rather rigid format. Rather, while you will of course have some introductory and concluding chapters, the substantive part of the thesis will be structured in the manner that provides the best exposition and development of your thesis argument.

There is no one right answer here—remember that any coherent thesis structure is acceptable and you do not have to adhere to any particular model. As long as you make sure that the structure offers the best exposition of your work then it will be acceptable. However, if you are working on a 'big book' style thesis you may wish to bear in mind how the thesis may be converted into a monograph and this may impact upon your choice of structure. Nevertheless, publication should be a secondary consideration—submission and successful defence is the key.

GOOD LEGAL WRITING

Good legal writing should share the same qualities as all good writing: it should be clear and precise. George Orwell, when not writing about dystopian futures or farmyard totalitarianism, was a harsh critic of poor writing. 'Good prose', he wrote 'is like a windowpane'. This (now somewhat trite) maxim applies to legal writing as much as it does to political writing or indeed to composition in any field. Unfortunately, for reasons unknown, many lawyers seem to revel in the self-conscious use of archaic English and redundant Latin. *Ergo*, their text becomes dense and difficult to read and *ipso facto* the meaning is obscured. *Res ipsa loquitur,* indeed. By being aware of how you write and attempting to write well it is possible to present your thoughts in a manner which not only makes your argument more clear, but which also makes it more compelling.

Fernando is a student from Argentina who had to adjust to the particular style of English legal writing. In doing so, he found adopting a new writing style was affecting the way he thought through and articulated his arguments: 'My main difficulty is that I am not a native English speaker. The way in which I would articulate my arguments is radically different from the English way. In Spanish we tend to use long sentences while English is more concise. This is proving a challenge for the way in which I am thinking through my work, even before I begin a draft. It took me a while, and lots of discussions with my supervisor to understand what my role was in legal scholarship and how I could express myself when analysing the law.'

Language and Vocabulary

Using the correct language and vocabulary is important for all good writing but it is particularly important for good legal writing. For example, if you are writing a thesis on the powers of the UK Parliament and you use the term 'parliamentary sovereignty' then it is important to note that that term and the concept it signifies has been the subject of much academic literature. You might be aware that the concept is sometimes referred to as 'parliamentary supremacy' but that the ideas of 'sovereignty' and 'supremacy' are not necessarily considered to be the same. If you decide to use one term or the other make the decision a conscious one and be aware of your reasons. If you decide that you are going to use the terms interchangeably then that may also be a valid academic choice, but beware that using such terms interchangeably may confuse some readers. Depending on the thesis it may make sense to specify those reasons in a footnote—or it may not—you need to decide for yourself. In general, while using a wide and varied vocabulary is a trait of good writing, it is important to use language consistently when technical terms are being discussed.

Beware the use of acronyms. These can be helpful as they prevent you from wasting words repeating long names such as the International Covenant on Civil and Political Rights (ICCPR) over and over again. However, too many acronyms can make the thesis hard to read. If you're writing about anti-money laundering and counter-terrorist finance (AML-CTF) carried out by the Financial Action Task Force (FATF) then sentences which refer to FATF

AML-CTF can begin to resemble complicated computer code. Sometimes the word count has to suffer to retain readability. The same is true for jargon more generally. While your supervisors are likely to be experts who will understand technical terminology, if you engage with broader discourses you may fall into the habit of using jargon that is unfamiliar to them. The result can be confusing and detract from the clarity of your thoughts. The use of inventive imagery or the occasional metaphor to illustrate a point can be helpful—adding some 'window-dressing' to Orwell's 'window-pane'. However, you should only use stylistic devices where they really do add value to your writing, not merely to show off how clever a composer of sentences you are.

Structure

A further aspect of good writing is having good structure *within* your chapters. Structure is about more than headings and sub-headings—each sentence, paragraph and section also has its own structure. Different sentence structures can be used to emphasise points and to make the reading experience easier. Having several short sentences in quick succession makes for a clipped reading style—swift but sometimes difficult to digest. On the other hand long sentences can also pose problems. If the reader has forgotten the start of the sentence by the time they have reached the end of it then it is unlikely that they will be able to process the ideas you are trying to convey. A good writer will vary the sentence length to allow for easy reading and quick comprehension. Paragraphs are also important. Each paragraph should have a purpose and that purpose should be furthered by the way in which you construct your paragraph. The obvious rule is that a paragraph should have a beginning and an end that introduce and conclude the thought contained in that paragraph. However, few writers can naturally write in this fashion and you may need to craft your paragraphs over time to ensure that your ideas are clear. While some authors recommend attempting to make paragraphs of equal length, this is not always possible and doing so simply for the sake of it is likely to lead you to either waffle on in some areas or over-edit in others. Paragraph length should only be dictated by the number of words and sentences necessary to convey your point—nothing more and nothing less. Don't be afraid to play around with your text. If you find that your writing isn't flowing as smoothly as you would like then try moving some sentences or paragraphs around. Sometimes a sentence that you write to introduce a thought will work better to conclude it.

Finally on structure, make sure that each paragraph in each section follows logically from the one that preceded it. One of the signs of confused academic writing is that each paragraph appears isolated from those around it. If this is the case then you will not be building an argument that proves (or disproves) a particular point, but instead you will be engaged in a scattered discussion of an eclectic collection of thoughts. One way to test whether your argument is flowing well is to take the first sentence (or first and last sentence) of each paragraph in a section and consider whether your meaning is clear from this sample of the section. Of course, the first sentence might be drafted to pique the reader's interest or to provoke a particular thought that you will then try to respond to. But the first and last sentence of a paragraph should between them give the reader a good idea of what that paragraph was about.

Knowing How Much to Write

It can often be difficult to determine just how much you should write on a particular idea. Within the 100,000 standard word limit for a doctoral thesis there is much discretion on how you compose your thoughts. On some occasions you may over-write a particular idea—giving over too many words or sentences to saying something that can be put more clearly and more directly. While Wilde was hardly thinking about law doctoral theses when he quipped that brevity is the source of all wit it can sometimes be useful to remember this advice when writing academically. Of course, with a thesis, there is also the risk of under-writing. Do not assume too much of your reader. You will have read far more about your topic than anyone else, including your examiners, by the time you have submitted your thesis. If you are unsure of the level of familiarity with basic concepts and terminology to assume of your examiners then ask your supervisor. You might also consider asking someone working in a closely-related, but distinct area of law to read your draft work. For example, if you're researching and writing about EU competition law then ask someone whose expertise lies elsewhere in EU law to read a chapter or two. If they consider the work to be too detailed or too closely argued then discuss with your supervisor whether you need to write more generally. There is no right answer here; you will need to discuss what is best in your case with your supervisor and other advisors.

Write, Edit and Re-write

We discussed the process of writing and re-writing in chapter four but it is particularly important during writing-up. Much of the writing you produced in earlier years may be edited out of the thesis during writing-up and this can be disheartening at first. One of the authors' favourite film reviewers, Mark Kermode, is fond of saying that a good director is one who is willing to 'cut his lovelies'—to relegate to the cutting-room floor scenes that were lovingly composed and shot. The same may (sometimes) be true of editing your PhD. You need to set your pride to one side and focus on producing the best possible report on your research. If this means excluding material that you slaved to draft two years previously then so be it. As we have mentioned elsewhere, these words will rarely go to waste and may form part of a separate article at a later stage.

PRODUCING THE FINAL DRAFT

Once you have revised each of the chapters in turn it will be time to return to the introductory and concluding chapters. These chapters are significant in terms of examination—a good introduction will capture the examiner's attention, give an overview of where the project fits within the academic literature and introduce the methodological approach to the study. Having read your introduction it should be clear to the examiner what sort of thesis they can expect to read in the pages that follow. The conclusion serves the same purpose at the end of the thesis. It should revisit the research hypothesis, summarise the outcomes of the research and any conclusions that can be drawn. The format of the final chapter will vary from thesis to thesis—it may be a few brief pages summarising the project or it may be a more substantive tract. Either way, by reading the introduction and conclusion it should be possible to understand what the project set out to investigate and the conclusions that it arrived at.

It is very important to proof-read your work. Of course, no matter how much you proof-read you are likely to miss the occasional spelling or typographical error. Nobody is perfect. However, a thesis that has been proof-read carefully will contain fewer errors than one that has not and the end product will look much more professional. If you are not the best at spotting misplaced apostrophes it may be worth your while asking a friend who is good at proof-reading to take a look at the thesis. Even the most eagle-eyed of us find it difficult to proof-read our own work and so having a second pair of eyes look at the completed work is always likely to be beneficial. Be aware that you are asking a lot of your friend and so it might help if you can offer to return the favour by proof-reading their thesis. Finally, when planning the days and weeks leading up to submission make sure to give yourself time in which to do this proof-reading—it can be an arduous task and you will not want to rush it. Having a week at the end of the writing-up period in which to complete this work will alleviate the stress involved in reading 100,000 words to look for wandering apostrophes.

More generally, it is important to avoid becoming too stressed during your writing-up period. We are not foolish enough to suggest that you don't become stressed at all—this period is the conclusion of a long and difficult research degree. Stress is therefore unavoidable. We discussed in chapter six the need to manage stress and that goes for writing-up stress as well. During this period you will be particularly prone to questioning the academic merit of your work. Don't! An important point to be borne in mind throughout the writing-up process and indeed throughout the whole research period is that you are not reinventing the wheel and nor are you required to. You will not produce the most profound work since *The Concept of Law* at the doctoral research stage of your career. It would be somewhat disappointing if you did—for if the best work of your career was produced at the very start then what would be the point in continuing? Even if you are capable of such profundity it is not required of you. Your thesis will not be perfect. Doctoral researchers tend to be perfectionists so this last revelation can be a difficult one to deal with. As long as you remember that your goal is to produce a work that can be defended in the viva then you will successfully complete your thesis.

If you haven't already done so, once you're working on the final draft you should choose a binding service (if you are required to bind your thesis). The rules and regulations on binding can be as arcane as those on formatting but most institutions will recommend a binding service that complies with the university's standards. Check how many copies you are required to submit and check how long it will take to turn your manuscript into a bound thesis. Many companies offer a sliding scale of prices depending on how quickly you need the finished product. You can save yourself some money if you can wait a little longer for the finished product—another incentive to make sure you complete your manuscript ahead of schedule. Approaching submission day you should double-check the paperwork that is required to be submitted with your thesis (if any). Also check the opening and closing hours of the relevant office at your university—imagine how awful it would be to bound up to the office door, thesis in hand, only to discover that you're 15 minutes too late to submit that day!

CONCLUSION

Writing-up may be the most difficult part of your degree. There will be days when you feel like the finish line is within touching distance and days when you feel like it's never been further away. To successfully make it through this challenging period you need to have faith in the work you have done to date and stick to a plan that will get you to your submission date. Keep the following points in mind:

— Seek out your institution's guidelines on how to format your thesis. Read and obey them.
— Devise a timeline to submission for your writing-up period. Having a clear path to submission will help you through the hard times.

— Structure your thesis in the manner which best makes your thesis argument. Discuss your structure with your supervisor and don't be afraid to reconsider your plan.
— Write clearly at all times and remember your primary audience: your examiners.

If you follow these guidelines you should find yourself with a completed doctoral thesis. Don't forget to reward yourself after submission—you've just reached the penultimate milestone on a long and arduous journey. After appropriate celebration you can turn your mind once more towards your thesis and the final milestone: the viva.

8

Examining the PhD

The examination of the PhD is the final obstacle to be overcome in your journey towards attaining the coveted 'Dr' title. Typically known as the viva (after the Latin *viva voce*, in living voice), the oral PhD examination is one of the least written about and understood aspects of the doctoral process. In the UK system the viva takes place behind closed doors with only the examinee and the examiners (and sometimes the supervisor) present. This is unlike the American or Continental European system where the viva (or defence as it is known in the US) is an open event which other academics, students and the examinee's family may attend—and in some cases even members of the public. The private nature of the UK-style viva makes it very difficult to provide an authoritative standardised guide to what to expect when you enter the examination room and close that door. And at the same time, it provides fertile ground for anecdotal horror stories to take root and flourish (that is not to say that they don't still occur, but contrary to what you might have heard, they are not the standard viva experience).

Each viva, like your PhD, will be unique. Nevertheless, in this chapter we try to provide, as far as possible, a guide to the common aspects of the viva process to help demystify the experience and make it as smooth as possible. The issues we address here are:

— What is the viva?
— The examiners: who are they and what do they do?
— General preparation for the viva
— What happens during the viva?
— Viva questions
— After the viva: what next?

By thinking about the viva in advance and speaking to former doctoral candidates you can take much of the mystery out of this part of the degree. Who knows, with luck your viva may turn out to be the most enjoyable part of the whole research process.

THE VIVA

The viva is the process through which you establish that you have met the criteria required for the award of the PhD. In chapter two, we referred to these criteria and it's worth revisiting them here. Typically they are that your thesis is:

— an independent piece of work which is a complete and coherent whole;
— forming a distinct contribution to the knowledge of the subject; either by
— the discovery of new facts and/or the exercise of independent critical power; which work is
— situated within the current literature of the field.

These should not come as any surprise to you; you should have become so familiar with these requirements during the course of your PhD that you can recite them off by heart (we don't recommend this as a party trick). It is during the viva that the examiners, who will have read your thesis beforehand, will be testing your ability to defend your work against these criteria. The viva also makes sure that the work that has been submitted was actually done by you, and that you understand and can justify the arguments made there. If you feel confident that you can meet all these criteria, and your supervisor has agreed that you are ready to stop writing and submit your thesis, then you are probably as ready as you can ever be to undergo the viva.

Law vivas tend to be shorter than those in the sciences and humanities, and usually last between 45 and 90 minutes. We have heard of vivas lasting much longer, but rarely are they shorter. If the viva is very long, then it may be broken up by five- or 10-minute breaks. The length of the viva does not necessarily indicate the strength or weakness of your work. We can recall a viva that took over three hours without there ever being any real doubt as to its successful outcome and another that took a mere 55 minutes—resulting in the student and examiners having to make small talk for another five to meet the institution's required one hour minimum! If the viva goes well then the time may fly regardless of how long it is—on the other hand a bad viva can feel like an age.

THE EXAMINERS

The role of the examiners is to make an independent assessment of whether you have met the criteria for the award of the PhD—this cannot be done by your supervisor. This assessment is made through questioning you about your thesis until they establish to their satisfaction that you have met these criteria. While this sounds rather nebulous, remember that the criteria for the award of the PhD are not subjective and mysterious, known only to the examiners. If you know the criteria, then you have a fairly good idea of what the viva and the role of the examiners entails.

A PhD usually has two examiners, one internal (that is, from your university) and one external to your university. The examiners should be experts in your general field and usually fairly senior academics. Sometimes there might be three, if one of the examiners is a practitioner rather than an academic. Where the examiners cannot agree (before the viva), a third examiner may also be brought in at the request of the first two to break the deadlock. Occasionally, depending on the subject of your thesis, an examiner may be brought in from outside the country. In some circumstances you may have two external examiners if this is justified by the thesis topic or the lack of availability of a suitable expert within the university itself.

The nomination of examiners is the task of your supervisor. In some situations your supervisor may involve you in that decision. If that is the case, then you should start thinking about potential supervisors very early on in the degree process. If there are people you think would be unsuitable, then speak up. If there are people you think would be eminently suitable, then speak up. Think about their work and how it relates to your research, and make sure you address it in the thesis. You do not want to find yourself being told that you have neglected to discuss the work of a very important academic (that is, the examiner) during the viva, when you could have checked off that issue well before submitting the thesis. But make sure also that any references that you do make are apposite and integrated into your work—no examiner will be impressed by a gratuitous and clumsy name-check.

On the other hand, you may have no input into the selection of your examiners. If this is the case, try to find out as much about them as possible before the viva. Read their work to establish whether they have any particular views on your subject. And if they are general experts (say criminal lawyers specialising in classification when your thesis is in defences) then think about how their interests might interact with the work you have done.

About six months before she was due to submit her thesis, Leilani had a meeting with her primary supervisor to discuss possible examiners. Her main goal was to make sure she didn't ask one particular person whose views Leilani strongly disagreed with—she was confident in her arguments but thought she would probably get an undeservedly hard time in the viva as a result. Leilani's supervisor immediately agreed not to ask that person. They spent the rest of the meeting talking about people that might be suitable. The PhD was interdisciplinary so they had also done some research into suitable people outside law. It was surprising how many people had to be excluded because they had co-taught or published with Leilani's supervisor. In the end her supervisor ended up approaching two people they hadn't discussed as several people on the list they had drawn up were over-committed and had declined. Leilani still thought the meeting was worth having to make sure she didn't end up with the one person she definitely didn't want.

Some people may be excluded from selection as an examiner on the basis of having worked too closely with you or your supervisor. Bear this in mind if you seek feedback on your work from academics other than your supervisors. Other conflicts of interest such as familial ties will also exclude certain potential supervisors.

When discussing potential supervisors it is worth remembering that while a good examiner is someone who engages in a rigorous but fair assessment of your work, a great examiner will stand you in good stead throughout your academic career. Some graduates go on to work with their examiners—co-authoring articles or organising conferences. Others will cite their examiner as a referee for publication purposes, grant or job applications. The best examiners take on a mentoring role of sorts and will direct you towards suitable conferences, help promote your work by recommending it (and you) to colleagues and provide useful counsel throughout your career. If you and your supervisor are confident about the merits of the thesis and its likelihood of passing then it is worth taking these broader considerations into account when selecting examiners.

Types of Examiners

Hopefully your examiners will be decent people and treat you accordingly. Your viva should be rigorous and challenging, yet ultimately enjoyable. It is after all, one of the few occasions in academic life you will have where your work gets individual attention at length from experts in your field. It may be the only occasion (or at least the only occasion for quite some time).

That said, sometimes less than ideal examiners do make their appearance at vivas. It's worthwhile thinking about how you would deal with someone in this category so that you are not taken aback if it does happen to you. Partington, Brown and Gordon (in Wellington 2005) provide a useful summary of some of these types you might encounter:

— The inquisitor—a confrontational examiner who fires out questions, often interrupting, and seeking to score points, intimidating rather than engaging with the student;
— The committee person—this examiner takes the thesis page by page rather than looking at it as a whole, denying the student the opportunity to discuss the key ideas of the thesis and its place in the discipline;
— The kite flyer—an examiner who has predetermined ideas about what the thesis is about (or should be about), effectively examining a thesis the student did not write;
— The reminiscer—the examiner who wants to spend the viva focusing on his or their research and publications, rather than examining the student's work;

— The hobby-horse rider—the reminiscer-type examiner with a particular agenda, who keeps on coming back to one theme or issue, often displaying a certain prejudice about those areas; and
— The proofreader—an extreme version of the committee type, an examiner who works through the thesis line by line, pointing out grammatical mistakes and typos.

If your supervisor has chosen carefully then you should not be subject to a grilling from any of this group. However, occasionally ordinarily good examiners have a bad day. If you find yourself with a difficult examiner remember that there are two examiners, not one, in the room. Be polite but firm in handling a difficult line of inquiry and take each question in turn. Try to stay (relatively) relaxed and, if necessary, don't be afraid to ask for a five-minute comfort break. We return to dealing with difficult questions below, but the war-time advice to 'keep calm and carry on' is a good rule of thumb when dealing with difficult examiners.

PREPARING FOR THE VIVA

The viva may well be the final examination of your academic education and as such you will want to prepare for it. As the culmination of three years' work it is not surprising that you will feel quite stressed and may find preparation difficult. Don't spend the entire time between submitting your thesis and the viva obsessively reading your thesis. You will benefit from taking a physical and mental break from being a doctoral student. Then, in the days before the viva, read, read and re-read your thesis. Make sure you not only know the key points of each chapter, but also that you know and can explain concisely how each chapter relates to the others to make a coherent whole. The day before your viva, stop!

Some time (usually three, but possibly up to six months) will have elapsed between the submission of your thesis and the actual examination. Make sure that you are up-to-date with any developments, legal or otherwise, that may have an impact on your thesis. Do the same with the legal literature.

Another useful preparatory exercise, if you can do so, is to find people who have been examined by your particular examiners. They may be able to give you important tips about the approaches of various examiners —do they take no prisoners? Are they the genial, supportive type? Do they take a broadbrush approach, or will you find yourself engaged in a 20-minute discussion of the permutations of the term 'legal pluralism' in footnote 201? Is there a question certain examiners are known for always asking?

As part of your preparation, think about the sorts of questions you might be asked, and what your responses might be. Cast a critical eye over your work. What is unique about your work? Are there any areas of weakness you could be probed on? What are the limitations of your thesis? Why did you choose a particular approach? Why did you look at this jurisdiction? This time period? It is very difficult, if not impossible, to predict exactly what questions you will be asked in the viva. You and your supervisor will have been involved with the work for three years or so and your perspectives on its merits and demerits will be coloured by your closeness to its development. Someone coming to the thesis with fresh eyes might find strengths and weaknesses you didn't and ask different questions as a result. Few of the questions you prepare for in advance are likely to arise in the viva. That's alright—the process of probing your work and practicing defending it is the key.

A mock viva is a very useful exercise to gain experience in defending your thesis. Not only does it take some of the tension out of the real event, but you get to try out your responses in a less-pressured environment. If you stumble on certain points, such as explaining why you chose a socio-legal rather than doctrinal approach, you can polish your responses so that when the time comes, a fluent answer is on the tip of your tongue.

Ask your supervisor if they are willing to put you through a mock viva. If you get a negative response, then try your friends, family, fellow students, and people you know who have recently graduated to help out. Encourage your mock examiners to be tough on you, so that when it comes to the real thing, you are not taken aback if you do get less than amenable examiners. Also think back to your upgrade experience or any times that you presented your work at a seminar or conference: what can you take from those experiences that you can apply to your viva?

However much you prepare for the viva you are still likely to be stressed on the day. Think about the logistics of the day in advance—how you will get to the venue and so on—and give yourself plenty of time so you're not under pressure. There's usually no set dress code for vivas. However, it is a very important moment in your life. We recommend you dress accordingly. Our tip: wear something dark (in case you spill anything on yourself, the stains won't show) and comfortable. You could be there a while, and the distractions of a tight collar or skirt are not what you need at this time.

IN THE EXAMINATION

Before the examination, the examiners should have independently prepared and exchanged reports on your thesis and set out their preliminary views as to the result. You and your supervisor do not have access to these reports beforehand, although usually you are given the preliminary reports after the viva. When you get the reports, you may well find that the viva itself affected the expected result. So do not discount the viva; it is a central part of the assessment process.

Helen is a respected professor in her field set to examine a doctoral thesis. Having read the thesis twice she had significant reservations about it—certain areas of the literature seemed to have been omitted, choices made by the candidate in their case studies were confusing and the thesis as a whole was less than convincing. Her preliminary report indicated that she suspected that addressing these concerns might require major revisions and a re-submission of the thesis. Upon examination however, Helen was pleasantly surprised. The candidate was able to explain both the omissions and the peculiar case selection choices. The problems with the thesis were less significant than they seemed at first. And following a hearty defence the examiners were able to recommend that the thesis be passed with minor corrections only.

This case demonstrates the very real value of the viva to a borderline candidate. The difference between major amendments and re-submission and minor corrections is significant.

Practicalities

The actual arrangement of the viva is the responsibility of your supervisor. He or she liaises with the examiners as to a suitable date (into which you may have some input) and arranges the venue.

The viva will probably take place at your home university. Some universities have special rooms that they use for vivas, whereas others will simply book any spare room. Vivas also often take place in supervisors' offices. A familiar environment may be comforting, but it may also mean you never feel the same about entering that room again. If the viva is being held in an unfamiliar venue, find out where it is beforehand. It is very rare for a viva to be conducted by tele-conference, video-conference or Skype but it can happen. If you are in this position (say, you have had to unexpectedly leave the country before your viva can take place or you were denied a visa to return for your viva) then make sure that you know how to use the technology appropriately and there is sufficient technical support available to you should things go wrong.

Do not expect the viva to take any set format. Even though the examiners will have met beforehand, discussed their approach to the viva and the questions they want to put to you, examiners may well bounce all over the thesis, and may not ask questions about some chapters at all. It isn't yet common in law, as it is in science vivas, for the candidate to start the viva with a short presentation, maybe even involving Powerpoint; you will have to find opportunities to present your work in its best light in other ways. You will usually be asked to introduce your work—by now you surely have a 5–10-minute overview off by heart from reciting it at various seminars and conferences during your degree.

You will be able to take a copy of your thesis into the examination room with you, marked up any way you like. You can also take in summaries of your thesis or chapter summaries. You should also take in notepaper and pen—these are useful for writing down those long or double-headed questions so that you don't get lost trying to answer them, and you can keep track of what was actually asked.

A common question students ask is whether the supervisor will be able to attend. Each university will have its own regulations on this point, and your supervisor may well have a personal policy on attendance as well. If your supervisor does attend your viva, bear in mind that supervisors are not usually permitted to intervene or assist in the examination in any way. On the other hand, if the viva goes badly, the presence of an independent third party as a witness can be invaluable.

Jake's viva experience was really tough. While he passed with minor corrections (adding in a reference to a case or two, and expanding on a point here and there) getting through the examination itself was gruelling. His supervisor attended the viva and Jake was grateful afterwards to have someone else who could confirm just how tough it actually was, even if he wasn't able to do anything about it at the time.

If you have any special requirements during the examination, make sure you communicate these early to your supervisor and the relevant university office. If you need frequent breaks for whatever reason, or specialist equipment such as an ergonomic chair set up to your specifications, then these should be arranged in advance. Check whether basics such as water will be available (and if not, bring your own)—an hour of answering questions without a drink can be thirsty work.

Dealing With Questions

We can't pretend that vivas are not a stressful experience. By its very nature, the fact that the award of a doctorate depends on your ability to explain and defend three years' or more worth of work to two senior experts in your area, the viva is going to be stressful. But try not to be overwhelmed by the occasion. You do know your work. You know it better than anyone else. You have been thinking about it for years, read all the literature, even dreamed about it on occasion (it will happen, it's inevitable). And, as a lawyer, you will most likely have had experience in mooting or other advocacy exercises of close scrutiny and questioning of your work which requires an oral defence—that's not to say that the viva will be a cross-examination, but there are similarities. Unless you have the misfortune of having hostile examiners, or ones with their own agendas, then the viva should be a robust, but friendly, discussion of your work with interested experts.

No matter how prepared you are, at some point you will be asked a question you don't know the answer to. Don't rush to cobble together an answer, or immediately capitulate and say 'I don't know'. Of course, if you genuinely do not know, do not try to bluff your way through a response. Don't allow yourself to get flustered. Take your time, and think about how best to respond. While taking a 30-second pause before answering may seem like a fatal weakness to you, in reality, it is hardly even noticeable. Saying 'that's a good point' is a useful technique—it serves the double purposes of flattering the examiner and buying you a little time. If you do stumble on a question, try not to let that throw your composure for the rest of the viva. Put it behind you and move on to the next one.

Remember that viva questions are not a one-way process. Try to establish a dialogue with your examiners. You too can ask questions: you can ask for clarification or for a question to be repeated or re-phrased. Don't be a passive recipient of the examiners' questions, but look for opportunities to turn their questions into a way to showcase your research and ideas. Be careful though, that you don't make the classic undergraduate mistake of answering the question you would have liked to have been asked or have prepared for instead of the one you were actually asked. Delivering a memorised answer will probably not help your cause. Finally, don't mistake probing questions for hostility to you or your ideas and respond in kind: that sort of approach will do you no favours.

Viva Questions

You might be surprised to discover that many doctoral graduates do not remember the questions asked during the viva. Maybe it's because the occasion becomes something of a blur in our memories. It's more likely that it's because a good viva will be less like a cross-examination and more like a discussion. A typical viva will begin with a question designed to put you at your ease and let the initial nerves settle. A common opener is 'how did you come to choose your topic?' This question lets you start talking without being under the pressure of thinking that your answer may be wrong, or full of hidden traps. The 'real' opening question in the viva is usually the one which asks you to explain how you have met the requirement of originality—one of the key criteria for gaining a doctorate. With this in mind, you can prepare an answer which sets out your thesis argument in its best light.

Rugg and Petre have an excellent summary of the types of questions commonly asked in vivas (Rugg and Petre 2004). Outside the 'throat-clearing' kind we mentioned above, they sort viva questions into the following categories:

— Confirmatory questions—here you can demonstrate your knowledge and mastery of your topic. A subcategory is the 'deep confirmatory question', allowing you to show just how well you know the topic, usually picking up on some aspect of your answer to a confirmatory type question;

— Calibration questions—these are more for the examiners, to allow them to check that they understand your work;

— 'Give me a reason to pass you' questions—these sorts of questions may probe your interpretation or arguments to enable the examiners to assess whether your work is of doctoral standard;

— Scholarship questions—these questions go beyond the boundaries of your particular topic, and check how well you know the field as a whole;

— Salvaging questions and redemptive questions—the type of question that lends you a hand, giving you an opportunity to re-phrase or re-argue a point that you may have expressed poorly or to admit to a mistake you have made and will want to avoid in the future;

— Pushing the envelope questions—these questions test the very boundaries of your knowledge;

— 'This is neat' questions—here, the examiner gets an opportunity to engage with your new and interesting ideas (don't be threatened by this type of question).

Of course, not all questions fit into a neat category and as we mentioned above, the ideal viva will develop into a conversation between you and your examiners about your work. Below, we have gathered some questions that have been asked in law vivas—just to make it clear that there aren't any super-secret lines of inquiry that are only pursued in viva exam rooms:

> Since your thesis is in the general field of cyberlaw, can you tell us why you have not covered this particular aspect of the subject?

> How do you think your work compares to that of Joseph Raz?

> How do you think that the work of Dworkin affects your arguments?

> What insights do you think can be applied from international humanitarian law to the arguments you are making in chapter two?

> Can you explain why you chose to structure your final chapter this way? I think it would have made more sense to have reversed these sections.

> What do you think the use of Derrida has added to your analysis?

> Can you speculate on future developments in this area?

> Consider the case of *Malone v Metropolitan Police Commissioner* on p108. Why do you think it was decided as it was? Can you explain why/how it was important to your thesis?

How do you think your arguments would help with the development of government policy in this area?

Why did you not include a further chapter developing the comparative conclusions from your various thesis chapters?

Don't be afraid to concede a point if it becomes clear that the examiners are right—or that you can't convince them that you are right. Knowing when your argument has been bested is an important part of academic debate. Some examiners will push a candidate until they utter the words 'I don't know' or 'I'm wrong'. This is not an act of sadism but an important test of the limits of the research.

Elaine's viva questions fell into two different categories. At the outset of the viva the questions were quite broad and helped settle her into the examination process. As the conversation developed the questions became more specific—probing the depths of her knowledge and checking certain points made in the thesis. Overall however the hour-long examination was more of a conversation than an interrogation. Afterwards she was able to relax and reflect with the examiners and her supervisor on the three-year research process which had now come to a final end.

If you find the discussion moving beyond what you can engage with based on your research project then say so—don't engage in speculation without at least qualifying your remarks. You can preface your comments with riders such as 'My work didn't examine that point, although it may be that...'. This allows you to continue the discussion while making clear that you know what you can and can't defend. At some point the viva will wind down, come to an end, and you will be asked to leave the room while the examiners confer as to the result. Regardless of how the viva has gone, these 10 minutes or so may well seem like the longest of your life.

AFTER THE VIVA

Hopefully when you are called back into the room, you will be given the examiners' verdict. Be aware though, that some examiners prefer to wait for the university to communicate the result to you in writing on the grounds that their role is only advisory—it is the university which has formal power to decide the result. If you are in this position, we can only sympathise. After years of work, waiting another few weeks to know the outcome can be agonising. More common though is for you to be told the outcome immediately. Essentially there are three outcomes: a pass, a conditional pass, or a fail. Within those categories, each university may have its own permutations, such as:

— Outright pass;
— Pass with minor corrections;

— Pass with major corrections;
— Referral and resubmission;
— Award of MPhil rather than PhD;
— Outright fail.

If you are fortunate to have been awarded your PhD without any further work being required, then sit on your laurels for a bit and enjoy your good fortune. If you find yourself in the unhappy position of not being awarded the PhD, reflect carefully on why that might have happened. People who find themselves here may have arrived at this point due to a breakdown in communication with their supervisor and/or submitted their thesis before it was ready without the supervisor's agreement.

If this is not the case, and you and your supervisor are confident that the thesis was of a passing standard, then consider whether you have any grounds for an appeal against the decision. You will be able to find details of the grounds for appeal and the process that should be followed in the relevant degree regulations at your university. For example, were you on the receiving end of maverick examiners who exhibited some sort of prejudice or bias against you or your topic during the viva? Or were there extenuating circumstances affecting your performance in the viva that were not taken into account? Or perhaps there were administrative errors or procedural irregularities during the viva that cast doubt on the result? If you think that any of these apply, then you should investigate your university's internal appeal processes. If you do go through an appeal and are unsuccessful, the next stage would be to make a complaint to the Office of the Independent Adjudicator for Higher Education. You cannot apply for judicial review of a PhD examination as academic judgements are regarded as being non-justiciable.

Whatever the outcome of the viva, there is likely to be necessary paperwork to be completed: a formal record of the viva, or the examiner's report, or some other institutional form to be filled. Your supervisor should take the lead in ensuring that examiners carry out their duties but you may wish to enquire in advance as to the correct procedure for the sake of your own peace of mind.

More Work To Do?

If, like the vast majority of PhD students, you emerge from the examination room with some extra work to do, then do not despair. Take a short break and then get down to work. You have come so far—doing corrections is a very small step towards the final goal.

In the case of major or minor corrections, typically you will be given six or three months to make the changes the examiners require. Make sure you know exactly what these are before you begin work. The examiners may tell you straight away what you need to do. If this is the case, unless they have simply handed you a sheet of typos you need to attend to, it would be wise to get written confirmation afterwards of what exactly needs to be done to meet their requirements. The alternative is that you receive a note after the examination setting out what you need to do. The approval of minor changes is usually delegated to your supervisor or your internal examiner, while major corrections typically need to go back to one or both of the examiners for checking.

If your thesis is referred, then it is even more important that you understand clearly what needs to be done. A referral means that the examiners believe that your work has the potential to meet the standard for a PhD, but is not quite there yet. You may need to rewrite certain sections to make your arguments clearer, sharpen your methodology, conduct more research to bolster your findings, or read more widely and show your engagement with the appropriate literature.

When the thesis is in its final approved state, it will need to be submitted to the university examinations office for deposit in the library. This can be an oddly anti-climatic experience. There is no crowd waiting outside to high-five you or put garlands around your neck. But celebrate anyway!

CONCLUSION

If not always the finish line, the viva is definitely the last lap of the PhD process. Like an Olympic marathon runner finishing a race how your viva goes will depend on how well you are doing. If you're doing well and the competition is already over then you should relax a little. If you have to battle through then do so—it will be over sooner than you may think.

Preparation is the key to feeling confident before the viva. Think through the sorts of questions you might encounter, try to have a mock viva, and make sure you are well rested and fed before you enter the examination room. Remember—the viva will be a unique and never to be repeated experience and so it's important to try to enjoy it if at all possible.

9

Publishing Your Work

As a PhD student, you may be so focussed on the work of researching and writing that you lose sight of some of the other aspects of PhD life. Although it may seem as if the PhD could, or might, stretch on forever, at some point you will finish. It is not a good idea to reach that point unprepared for what comes next. While you are working on your thesis, you also need to be thinking about life after the thesis. This requires you to give some thought to where you want to be and how to get there. Part of that preparation involves networking, teaching, getting involved in research communities, and, if appropriate, gaining experience outside academia. These are addressed in the next chapter. Here we look at the issues surrounding the publication of your work:

— Why should I publish my work?
— What should I publish?
— Where should I publish?
— Publishing from your thesis.

Publishing during your PhD gives you a taste of what academic life is like, but can seem like a daunting task when you first attempt it. This chapter aims to demystify the publication process by explaining the path from draft to printed text.

WHY YOU NEED TO PUBLISH

There are many reasons why you should publish your work. Some of them are personal, including the sense of achievement and the warm glow you will experience when you see your name in print. You might also get some personal satisfaction from seeing your writing skills improve over the years as you transition from a novice to a seasoned expert. But for most writers, these are not the primary drivers for publication, rewarding though they may be.

If you intend to have a career as a law academic, publishing is an inescapable expectation of the job. Like all aspects of the academic role, writing for publication is a particular skill, and one which you can improve on throughout your career. It makes sense to start practising those skills early. While there's no magic number of publications necessary to secure a job most universities will expect you to demonstrate some sort of track record before hiring you. This may vary from a single article in a good peer-reviewed journal in some institutions to having your doctoral thesis under contract at others. Obviously the more competitive the jobs market the more employers can expect of applicants. In the UK, research universities will expect you to be thinking about their Research Excellence Framework (REF) submission—which currently means having four publications in each assessment cycle. However, this area of university life is forever in flux and attitudes vary from university to university so it's hard to be too prescriptive about what is expected of new academics.

Why are academics expected to publish? Being an academic is about contributing to knowledge: pushing the boundaries of legal wisdom, offering new interpretations or a critique of existing law, explaining the social consequences of law, and bringing new ideas or ideas from other disciplines to inform the development of legal thinking and the law. In order to achieve these goals, people need to be aware of your ideas. The way this is done in academia is primarily through publication (speaking at conferences or participating in media debates are other, but more transitory, ways). In addition, publishing your ideas gives you a claim to ownership of them. It is no good having plenty of useful and insightful thoughts if you never articulate them. Someone else may also be having those thoughts and be able to take the credit for them by publishing first. Contributing to the academic debate by publishing your thoughts can also help drive the debate forward. You and others will benefit from active engagement with each other's work. If each scholar simply sat and worked in isolation progress would be much slower. Publication also serves the connected purposes of building your profile as a researcher, and establishing your place in the community of legal scholars. As your profile builds, so should your career progress.

WHAT TO PUBLISH DURING YOUR PhD

Your primary focus during your studies should of course be the writing of your thesis. But sometimes an opportunity for publication arises that shouldn't—or couldn't—be resisted. Getting some publications on your CV is important, particularly if you intend to go into academia, as they demonstrate your potential as a scholarly writer.

Case-notes, legislation-notes, book reviews and recent development reporting are popular choices for PhD students. They are usually short, do not take much time, and can often be combined with your doctoral work. A case-note is a critical examination of a recent judgment (or of a Bill or new Act for a legislation-note). It offers the opportunity to engage in debate and to throw out some ideas without having to develop them to the same extent as would be expected in an article. A good case-note may become frequently cited as the go-to reference for a discussion of the case that is critiqued. In some, but not all, cases the review process for case-notes is less onerous and so publication may be swifter and a more gentle experience.

Book reviews may be even more straightforward. A book review may vary from 500 to several thousand words and is designed to critique the ideas in a recent publication. Reviewing books can be an easy way to gain experience with the publication process but at this stage of your career you must be careful. The level of critique in book reviews can vary widely. Often, the sign of a bad review is the absence of fulsome praise rather than anything explicitly negative. Authors are understandably touchy about bad reviews and you don't want to alienate a potential examiner! Read a few book reviews before you write one and seek to have your work checked by a more experienced scholar to help you avoid shooting yourself in the foot.

A final option may be available if your university has an in-house law review. If so, it might be worth seeing if you can contribute to a 'recent developments' section. You will probably not get a credit for each individual contribution you make, but you will be able to put your position on the journal on your CV. And it's a very handy way of keeping up with the law.

If you wish to write something more substantial there are a number of options available to you. Sometimes you may have written up some work as part of your studies that can't be fitted into your thesis. Don't discard it. Instead see if you can refashion it into a journal article. Another option is to prepare a conference paper that is based on work done during your thesis— many conferences publish their proceedings and invite presenters to submit their papers for consideration for a book based on the proceedings. If you attend a conference that does not offer publication then you might choose an appropriate journal and submit it for consideration.

You may simply need a break from your thesis and decide to write about something else for a change. Writing in a different area can be a welcome breath of fresh air but you should always remember that your principal concern is completing your thesis: don't stray too far away for too long!

Robin was in the second year of his PhD and had just handed in a chapter to his supervisor when the House of Lords delivered a judgment in a fascinating case. The decision was all over the newspapers; otherwise he probably wouldn't have been aware of it, as it was in an area Robin hadn't paid much attention to for years. He quickly wrote up an extended case-note that focused on an unusual aspect of the decision. Robin submitted it to the top journal in the area and to his amazement, it was accepted. He even had the head of the body referred to in the judgment contact him for a copy. Even though it was only a case-note, in all his job interviews after he had finished his PhD, the interview panels would comment on the fact that he had a publication in this very well-known journal.

WHERE TO PUBLISH YOUR WORK

Your ideas can be published in a variety of places. The development of the internet in particular has opened up the horizons significantly—you can publish short pieces on blogs or other websites, and there are also opportunities for publication in departmental newsletters, in practitioner journals or websites, and in law student magazines. You may even be able to secure a position writing opinion pieces for your local newspaper.

Nonetheless you should not seek to build a career solely on brief commentaries. The gold standard in academia is the article in a scholarly journal or law review. Publishing in such a forum is a clear sign of your potential as a scholar. This is not mere snobbery—academic journals will usually be edited by leading scholars and contributions will be peer reviewed. This process is discussed further below. It represents confirmation your work has met the standards of the academic legal community and contributes in a real and meaningful way to the debate in your field.

Academic journals

Law journals fall into two types: the subject specific and the general. Which category a journal falls into can usually be worked out from its title. For example, *Legal Studies*, the *University of Toronto Law Journal*, the *Harvard Law Review* and the *Modern Law Review* are all generalist journals. The *International and Comparative Law Quarterly*, the *Criminal Law Review* and the *Carbon and Climate Law Review* are subject specific journals. Journals may also be focussed around a particular perspective, such as the *Yale Journal of Law and Feminism*, the *Journal of Comparative Law* and *Jurisprudence*.

Which Journal?

Targeting the right journal for your work plays a large part in the success of a submission. Many pieces are rejected straight away because they are simply not suitable for the journal they were sent to—prospective authors having ignored the perspective of the journal, its jurisdictional focus, or its length stipulations. It may seem obvious, but paying attention to the fit between your work and the journal will pay dividends in the long run.

The first step in narrowing down the appropriate journal is to be aware, if you are not already through years of reading journal articles, of the range of journals in your subject area. Your supervisor and academic peers may also be able to suggest suitable candidates. Then look through the bibliography for your thesis. Do the same half-dozen journals keep appearing? Finally, check a ranking service (see below). This may help you identify possible journals you haven't encountered yet, but which may also be suitable. Don't restrict yourself to journals in your own jurisdiction—you may find a suitable home for your work in a foreign law journal.

Once you have identified the suitable candidates for your work, you need to become familiar with the journal's criteria for submission. These are usually entitled 'Notes for Authors' or 'Notes for Contributors' and should be prominently located on the journal's website or in the back pages of each issue. These are very important and you ignore them at your peril. The Notes for Authors will cover issues such as the types of submissions the editors are interested in receiving, the expected length, the style guide to be adopted and whether exclusive submission is required. A note about exclusive submission— while you can theoretically submit your piece to several journals at once, we don't recommend this unless you are specifically told it is acceptable (this is more common in the case of US-based journals). Ignoring the rules on exclusive submission wastes editors' time if they make you an offer, only to see you withdraw your piece because it was accepted elsewhere, often tries the patience of referees (in a small field, your submission may be sent by several editors to the same referee) and as a result can make you unpopular within the academic community.

You will probably have some idea of the relative standing of the journal you are thinking of submitting to. The status of the journal is an important consideration because it acts as a default indicator of the quality of your work and thereby your profile and standing. Not many people may read your work, but they will all know what it means when you say 'I just published in the *Law Review Everyone Wants to Publish In*' rather than 'My piece appeared in the *Obscure and Unknown Law Journal*'.

But how do you go about finding out where journals stand in relation to one another? This is a rather contentious issue. There have been attempts to provide comprehensive rankings of law reviews but it's best to take these as a guide only rather than gospel.

There is no specific rankings list for UK journals. The two that are the best known in the common law are the Washington and Lee Law Review Rankings and Submissions database (www.lawlib.wlu.edu/LJ/index.aspx) and the Australian Research Council rankings (www.arc.gov.au/era/: this includes all disciplines, not just law). The Washington and Lee rankings are US-focussed, although other jurisdictions can be searched. These rankings are centred on citations. Each journal is monitored annually to see what citations to its articles are generated, be it in articles published in other journals or in cases. Also checked are how quickly citations begin after publication, and the total number of citations (this is known as the impact factor). Details of the ranking methodology including the weighting given to each aspect of citations can be found at the website. The Australian Research Council methodology is rather less transparent. Washington and Lee rankings are numerical, while the Australian Research Council puts journals into categories from A* to C.

Opinion is divided as to how high you should aim. One school of thought is that you should not aim too high, as rejection can be crushing and there are gentler ways to become acquainted with the world of law reviews. Others adopt the view that you might as well aim for the very top—if that journal rejects your work, then there are plenty more to choose from to resubmit to once you have done some reworking. You may also surprise yourself and achieve the academic version of a hole in one from the first tee. We are optimists, and tend to the second point of view.

The Submission Process

Before you send off your paper, it can be worthwhile making a preliminary inquiry of the editor to see if there is any interest in receiving it. This is especially useful if you have written on something very topical: an editor may already have received an article on that exact subject. If you receive a favourable response (or at the very least, you don't receive an outright rejection) then you should send in your piece. These days this is usually done electronically, although you will find a few editors still prefer to receive a hard copy accompanied by a disk. You can also use a submission service like LexOpus or ExpressO to submit your work (this is particularly useful if you are making several simultaneous submissions). As the name implies, submission services do the work of submitting your article for you. You upload your article to the service's website, and from there it is sent to the journals you've indicated. You can then electronically manage your paper post-submission, making revisions, withdrawing it altogether, requesting expedited consideration, and checking its progress. Editors may also be able to see how far along in the process your article is with other journals.

Once your article arrives on the editor's desk, the first sifting process takes place. This is where most articles that will be rejected fail. The editor, or another member of the editorial team, will take a quick look at your submission and form a preliminary view as to whether it should be sent out for review. Articles which don't go any further may have failed to meet quality standards (usually by being too descriptive or simply incomprehensible) or they may be outside the scope of what that particular journal would consider publishing. This is why it is important to maximise your chances of going forward by paying close attention to any available guidance.

If the editor thinks that your work is probably publishable, then it will be sent out to one or more referees for their expert opinion. This process usually proceeds on a 'double blind' basis. This means that your work will be anonymised (by the editor, but you can help by not including self-references or other clues to your identity such as citing your own work) before being sent out, and the identity of the referees will also not be disclosed to you. This practice should ensure that your work is assessed on its merits alone.

What do Referees Look for?

The short, if unsatisfying response to the question 'what do referees look for?', is that they are evaluating your work for its suitability for publication. This assessment process has a number of criteria. Some journals make these explicit to their referees while others simply ask for an assessment in the round.

Typically, referees will be looking at the following areas: the originality of your argument; the contribution you make to the literature on the topic (is this a topic of current debate? are you challenging orthodox understandings? has anything been written on this topic before?); and the depth and quality of your research. Referees also look for readability, structure, and general punctuation and style issues. You may have written a well-informed critique of the Supreme Court's latest judgment on pre-nuptial agreements, but if you have expressed yourself poorly, then you're unlikely to have your work accepted.

This process can take a varying amount of time. Academics act as referees as part of their general professional responsibilities and so the work is unpaid. As a result, devoting time to your article may not be their immediate priority. If you haven't heard back within six weeks or so, then it's acceptable to send a polite inquiry to the editor about the fate of your submission. Eventually, the referees will respond to the editor with their views, and one of three recommendations: accept without revisions, revise and resubmit, and reject without further revision.

Revise and Resubmit or Rejection?

Having your work accepted untouched is fairly uncommon. It is much more likely that the referees will come back with suggestions for improvement. Although this can be an unsettling experience, try to look at it positively—an expert in the area has looked at your work, and is making suggestions to help make it better. If this is the outcome, respond promptly to the editor, thanking the referees for their time and input, and assure the editor that you will get to work on the suggestions and return the piece by the expected deadline. If the referee says that your argument is unclear in places, then work on your clarity of expression. If you need to provide more examples to strengthen your point, then find them. If your work needs re-structuring to make the argument flow more smoothly, then think about how you can do that.

That said, you do not have to agree with everything that the referees say. Often referees' suggestions reflect their own particular biases and interests. These may not align with yours. Sometimes accommodating all the suggested changes can turn your work into something quite different from what you had originally set out to do or derail a section of your argument and upset the flow of the piece. In responding to the editor, you are entitled to question some of the referees' suggestions and make the case for why you think your paper would be better in its original form. You can agree with the editor to incorporate some suggested changes and to omit others. An alternative strategy is to deal with the referees' concerns in a less fulsome way than the referees might have envisaged. A simple reference to the point with a footnote acknowledging that while this is an important and relevant concern, it is 'beyond the scope of this paper' can often work.

Even if your work is rejected outright, do not give up on your piece. Look at the referees' comments and see if there is anything you can salvage from your work. It may be that it is more suited to being published in a practitioners' journal than a scholarly one. Or perhaps it would fare better as a case- or legislation-note than a full-length article. Sometimes, it may just be that a referee was having a bad day and rejected your article out of grumpiness. If you have read all the comments and still believe that the criticisms were unwarranted (and be very honest with yourself when you do this) then try submitting it elsewhere—you may find that another journal and another referee on a different day can help your article find its proper home.

Natalya co-wrote an article with another student on some new developments in solicitors' disciplinary hearings and sent it to an overseas journal for their verdict. The editors were initially very encouraging, but when the referee's report came back, it was awful. It was only three lines long, and said that the article was boring and 'contributed nothing new'. Natalya and her co-author just couldn't see how this was the case. They knew this topic hadn't been covered before but they also weren't in a position to tell the editors the referee was being unreasonable. A few months later they saw a call for papers from a journal putting together a themed issue. The students re-wrote parts of the article to mesh with the theme and sent in the piece. This time the referee said how interesting and novel it was, and it should definitely be published! While it's hard to know if it was the original ideas or themed version of the article that merited publication, Natalya realised that when it comes to publishing a good piece is worth another throw of the dice.

As you progress through your career you will become more adept at having your work accepted by academic journals. In part this will be because you have become a better scholar, but also because you will have become accustomed to the conventions of participating in the academic discussions in your area of research.

PUBLISHING FROM YOUR THESIS

When the viva is over and the final copy of your thesis is filed, your first instinct may well be to never look at your thesis again. Obey that instinct—for a little while. Then after a few weeks or even a month or so, revisit your thesis and start to think about how it can continue to work for you.

What to Publish?

There are a number of ways you can publish from your thesis. You can slice your thesis into a number of separate articles and have each one published in a law review. Or you can extract one or two major pieces as articles and set the rest aside (this may be a better option if your thesis resembles a social sciences PhD, with separate methodology and literature review chapters). Another option, if your thesis deals with two discrete topics that you have brought together, is to split them up and work each one up into a book.

The typical publication route for a law thesis remains to try to have it published in its entirety, as a monograph. A monograph is a specialist academic work of scholarship (as opposed to a textbook or a general reference book). What are the steps in seeing your thesis become a book? Do not expect that your thesis can be transformed into a book simply by sending it off to a publisher and getting a new cover put on it. A book and a thesis have many things in common but they are not the same. It is quite likely that your thesis will need some revision before it can be considered a book. William Germano, in *From Dissertation to Book*, provides a useful comparison of their differences which we have adapted here (Germano 2005).

Thesis	Book
Fulfils degree requirements	Fulfils desire to address broader audience
Your examiners are the audience	The academic community is the audience
Usually up to 100,000 words	Length depends on publisher and market
Structured to demonstrate analytical skills	Structured to demonstrate narrative
Often fewer, longer chapters	Usually several, shorter chapters
Stops	Concludes

In essence, a thesis is a piece of writing designed to satisfy particular academic conventions and written for only a handful of people to read. In a thesis, you need to show that you have met the criteria for a PhD. This is often done quite overtly, with lots of signposting ('In this next chapter I will show'; 'The methodology I have adopted is a socio-legal one'; 'As I demonstrated in the previous chapter') and conscious referencing of your sources to demonstrate the depth and breadth of your research. A book does not need these features.

Where to Publish?

The thesis book is usually the first book published by a scholar and so it is important to do the job right. Avoid vanity publishers. These are publishers who will accept your work without any revisions and most likely, charge you a fee for publication. Quick-fix publication may be tempting, but it will do nothing for your academic prospects and more likely, will harm them. Similarly, do not be tempted to publish your thesis yourself (say, by putting it up on the web and telling everyone you have published your thesis electronically). Self-publication may have worked for Nietzsche, but unless your genius is also gravely underestimated, this sort of approach will be seen as a particularly embarrassing form of vanity publishing.

Submitting Your Thesis to a Reputable Publisher

If you are committed to publishing your thesis with a reputable publisher you need to prepare yourself for an often long process of writing and waiting. Just as in the case of law reviews, it is worthwhile approaching potential publishers to gauge whether there is interest in receiving your work. How do you know which publisher to approach? Your examiners may have mentioned possible publishers during your viva. If so, this can be useful to mention when approaching them. It helps especially if your examiners or supervisor can provide the name of an actual person that you can contact. Your university may have its own publishing press, and may look favourably on the work of its graduates. Look also at the journals you regularly refer to: some are published in-house at university law schools, but others are published by publishing houses. You will also be familiar with the leading publishers of law books from your own research: check out their websites and see whether they welcome the submission of doctoral theses. Think about whether you want to approach a specialist law publisher, a general publisher with a legal division, or a general academic press.

As well as identifying a publisher, you also need to think about the sort of publisher you want for your book: the readership, the reach of the publisher (will it be domestic or international), and the prestige. Each publishing house has something different to offer, so do some research into whether what they offer fits with your aims for your book.

Once you have decided on a publisher to send your manuscript to, as with law review submissions, pay careful attention to the proposal requirements. You will find these on each publisher's webpage. As a general guide, proposals need to address the following topics:

— Your biographical details
  Who are you? What is your background and why are you best placed to write this book?
— A summary of the monograph
  What is this book all about? What is the general area? What is its central argument? Is it international, comparative, or domestic in focus? How long do you expect it to be?
— A proposed table of contents
  What are the details of the book? How are the chapters structured and what do they contain?
— The intended audience
  What sort of people would be interested in buying this book? Is it suitable as a student text? Could it be sold to practitioners? Is it a niche work? Will potential buyers be found outside legal circles?
— Other books in the area
  What is the competition for your work? What is unique about your work that means a publisher should take it on?

It's also wise to submit a couple of sample chapters, as well as the examiners' reports (particularly if they make favourable comments about publication). One seemingly small task that requires a disproportionate amount of your attention is the potential title. Thesis titles tend to be either long and descriptive ('A comparative analysis of bilingual court reporting in New Zealand and Wales: 1990–2010') or a combination of long and descriptive prefaced with a punning or popular culture-referenced title ('War! What is it good for? An investigation into the crimes of art and antiquities theft in the aftermath of the Iraq War'). Neither of these approaches is going to work for a book. Think about the big picture of your thesis and try to express that succinctly but in an interesting way in the title. Many people now find books through internet search engines so working out what are the key words that express the core of what your book is about can stimulate ideas for an appropriate title.

If your proposal catches a publisher's interest, the next stage is to send the proposal (and sometimes some sample chapters) out to an external referee. This is a very similar process to that for a journal article. If the referee takes a favourable view, then the publisher (or commissioning editor in a larger house) will take your proposal to the board for their approval to offer you a contract. If you get an unfavourable review, as with a journal article, think about what use you can make of the referee's points, go to work on them, and resubmit your manuscript to another publisher.

Revising Your Thesis

If your thesis is accepted by a publisher, congratulations! Now comes the work of revising your thesis. The extent to which you revise your thesis depends in part on how quickly the law and legal debate in your area is developing and the amount of time you are willing to invest in further developing your work on this project. There are two types of revision you will have to make. How deeply you have to immerse yourself in each will depend on the state of your thesis.

The first type of revision is somewhat superficial but is essential to the publication process. You will need to remove all references to the previous life your manuscript had as a thesis. This includes all the times you have written 'This thesis' or 'as part of my research' as well as the other features of the thesis (the abstract, the acknowledgements page, and the like) that have no part in a book. Remove all the signposting. While this was necessary to prove to the examiners that you had proposed an argument, worked through it, and had concluded on it, in a book your argument should stand by itself without these indicators. Readers do not need to be told exactly what is happening at each point in the narrative; if you have done your job well, that should be obvious.

You should also tackle the issue of what William Germano calls 'dissertation style' (Germano 2005). This he sums up (rather pessimistically) as exhibiting the following features:

— an overdependence on citation and reference;
— an effortful attempt to sound very professional, which comes out sounding stuffy;
— repetitious statements of intent (signposting);
— an overuse of the passive voice and elaborate sentence construction; and
— either an unseemly pompousness or a willed lifelessness, as if being a professional scholar meant showing as little expression as possible.

Take a long look at your thesis, and ask yourself exactly what purpose the words on the page are serving. Could you have expressed yourself more clearly, more concisely? Is your tone artificial or too formal? Have you peppered your writing with jargon? Does the general but well-informed reader need all those footnotes? Does your argument need those quotations to make your points, or can your arguments stand alone? If appropriate, at this stage you can probably also cull any stand-alone literature review and/or methods chapters. This sort of material can be re-integrated into your manuscript when you get to the next stage.

The other sorts of revisions you need to consider are the ones that go to the heart of the transformation process: more than just making your thesis *look like* a book, now it should *become* a book. It is at this stage that the external readers' reports come into play: they may have suggested the shortening of a section, the introduction of new material, making one argument more prominent, and another less strong.

First, take a look at your introduction. Many theses spend time in the introduction setting out exactly how their coverage or approach is different and unique. This is not unexpected as it is of course a requirement for the degree. But in a book you do not need to spell out why your work is superior or new—that will be evident as the chapters progress. Moreover, you do not need to fill space with apologias for what you did not do. Statements like these are not needed:

> I did not touch on the question, important though it is, of whether cats are entitled to rights on the same basis as humans. Instead I chose to focus on the related issue of whether dogs are entitled to these rights. This limitation of my research is justified by a severe allergy to cat dander which prevented me from doing the necessary empirical research into this particular area.

No book can cover everything and no reader will expect you to. What you have chosen to write about can stand on its own two feet as a topic of interest. Your introduction may need to provide a more general background to your subject to explain the context and hook your readers' interest; it may need cutting for the same reasons. Next, look at the body of the thesis. What your thesis will need as part of the transformation will depend on its present state.

First, address the suggestions of the publisher's referees. This may involve changing the structure or making changes to the content. Chapters may disappear or merge together, or may be shifted from one section to another. Be open to their suggestions rather than defensive. Likewise, with the content, be prepared to say goodbye to that section that you thought was critical to your thesis, but which in the cold light of day after the viva, you can admit was actually self-indulgent, or to remove that section that had to go in there because you couldn't quite bear not to show that you had done that research, really you had. You may also have to add in new material, particularly if there have been new developments in case law or elsewhere. These in turn may affect some the points you made in your earlier writing.

You also need to think about the overall narrative drive of the manuscript. What is the journey you are taking the reader on? How do the words pull the reader along the path you have set out? Is your writing logical, clear, and interesting? And what is your voice in all of this? If you are still hiding behind the words of others or resting on too many quotations, then stop. It will be your name on the front of the book, so make sure that the readers hear you, not dozens of other scholars, as they read.

If you have chapters you set aside at the first stage revisions, then this is the point to think about whether they have a place in the book. General readers do not need to have your chosen methodology explained and justified to them. Similarly, they do not need to be taken on a journey through all the writing on which you are using as a springboard for your work. Try to integrate this material into your manuscript in a less obvious way so that it becomes a natural part of your work.

The revisions process is essentially one of re-thinking and re-writing. You may prefer to tackle the entire thesis at once. A good way of doing this is to print out the table of contents, and then begin cutting and pasting it into a different order (with additions and subtractions where necessary). Then the re-writing can commence. Or you may like to work systematically through the thesis, changing each chapter on its own, and then dealing with the consequential changes down the line as you come to them.

Lastly, when all the revising is done, set the manuscript aside for a while. When you come back to it, read it in one go as if it were the book it is going to become. Ask yourself whether there is any more work to be done or if you can send it back to the publisher. It is possible to make small changes after you have submitted the manuscript to the publisher, first at copy-editing stage, then again at proofreading stage. However, publishers are likely to stress that only essential changes should be made post-submission and it is best to regard the manuscript as final once you have submitted it to the publisher. Do be vigilant for little changes in the copy-editing that may change the nature of your argument—the omission of a 'not' could make all the difference. Once you've dispatched the manuscript you can consider yourself well on your way to publishing your book.

CONCLUSION

As a doctoral student, your life will revolve around research and writing. Publishing is the reward for good writing and a necessary part of academic life. Your doctoral monograph is unlikely to be the first time you publish, but it is the chance to finally close the book on your PhD (pardon the pun) and is a wonderful way to send the thesis out into the world. Though it may at times be a frustratingly slow process it is worth it in the end.

10

Building a Career

The previous nine chapters have been devoted to the process of conducting doctoral research in law—from first applying to the programme to defending your research and publishing the thesis. In this, our final chapter, we consider the wider question of building a career in academia. Here we focus on a career in academia as that is the principal destination of law doctoral graduates in the UK. If you do not want to pursue a career in the academy—as a significant proportion of graduates do—you may wish to return to chapter one to consider the other options that are available to you. For broader careers advice, you should get in touch with the careers office at your university. Here we consider:

— teaching and research;
— the need to network; and
— presenting a conference paper.

There are many career resources available. Our focus is on the relationship between the doctoral research degree and the academic career. Life in universities appears to have been undergoing a permanent revolution these past few years and there is no end to the changes in sight. Speak to your supervisor, recent graduates of your doctoral programme, and the more junior staff members in your institution for an idea of the trials and tribulations of building an academic career in the early twenty-first century. And remember: academic careers happen as much by accident as they do by design. Some of the most interesting opportunities will be the ones that fall in your lap rather than those you actively seek. Weigh each opportunity carefully and decide what is best for your own development.

TEACHING AND RESEARCH

If you want a career in academia—especially in law—then you will spend at least some of your life teaching. In other academic disciplines it is possible to build a career through research alone. As much activity in a modern law school still revolves around training the next generation of lawyers it is unlikely that you will be able to escape the classroom for too long. As a result, those recruiting new members of staff will expect you to have obtained some teaching experience during your doctoral degree. Teaching experience varies—from giving a guest lecture or seminar on your supervisor's course to running an entire course of your own based on your research. The type of teaching experience you secure will depend on how advanced you are in your career, your research field and your institution's needs. If you are fortunate enough to be based in a large city with several universities then there will be even more opportunities to teach, though you should bear in mind that institutions are likely to favour their own students and graduates when allocating part-time or casual teaching.

Although it is quite important to obtain teaching experience during your degree you should not let your teaching commitments take up all of your time at the expense of your research. Teaching takes time, not just the relatively modest hours you might spend in the classroom, but also the considerable time it can take to prepare for class, mark assessments, deal with student queries and address the plethora of other administrative duties that may accompany a teaching position. As a result we do not recommend that you seek teaching experience during the first year of your doctoral research when you need to focus entirely on establishing the scope of your research project. Teaching experience is best obtained in the middle of your degree when you are more certain of the direction of your research but have not yet begun the difficult process of writing-up your thesis.

You will need to decide *what* to teach. Depending on your research interests you may or may not be able to contribute to one of the 'core' undergraduate subjects in law degrees: public, criminal, contract, EU, property, tort, equity and trusts. These subjects are offered on almost all law degrees and therefore being able to teach one or more of them will help you to get teaching experience during your doctoral research degree and to secure a job afterwards. Even if you do not research in one of these areas any experience you can secure in teaching one of them will stand you in good stead. Outside of the core subjects you need to be more judicious in choosing your teaching subjects. Teaching an optional subject on an undergraduate or taught postgraduate degree should only be considered if there is a clear link between your research and the subject. It is simply not an efficient use of time for someone conducting PhD research on TWAIL (Third World Approaches to International Law) to teach UK administrative law. The students may expect a greater degree of expertise from a teacher on an optional subject and the teaching delivery is likely to be through more intensive seminars. As a result, the time taken to prepare and the lack of an opportunity to air your research ideas in class can make this form of experience more trouble than it's worth.

Even if you are one of the fortunate few students who are presented with the opportunity to teach a specialised course on their research area you should still think carefully before accepting. While we would generally advise students to take these opportunities there is still a time cost in preparing classes and that cost must be borne in mind. Obviously if the teaching is limited to one or two seminars as part of a larger course organised by someone else then you should jump at the opportunity. But if you will be required to design the course, organise its delivery and draw up and mark examinations then you should weigh the benefit to your career against the cost to your doctorate. If you decide it is a worthwhile venture—which it often will be— you will need to manage your time carefully. We have encountered several examples of good researchers whose doctorates have fallen victim to their desire to gain teaching experience and secure a livelihood. Part-time teaching should only ever be a stepping-stone to a more secure career—if you stay as a casual employee for too long you may find it becomes more and more difficult to move on.

Paul's doctorate was in the area of EU law and as a result he was able to secure EU law teaching at no fewer than three universities during the third year of his doctoral degree. While this left Paul in a very good position financially, he struggled to balance his research and teaching commitments. On an average term-time week he would spend 11 hours in the classroom—far more than most full-time academics would. In addition he had mountains of course-work to mark and as a result could only work for a day or two a week on his research project. Despite his commitment to these institutions, when Paul applied for a permanent position at one of them he was unsuccessful. The department passed him over for someone whose research interests were more closely related to those of the existing staff. Paul has since completed his doctorate and obtained a full-time position elsewhere, but his experience is a good reminder that an institution's needs are not always the same as those of their staff or students and you must protect your time if you are to complete your doctorate and build your career.

If you do engage in teaching you will want to do as well as you can. Apart from the satisfaction of a job well done, good student feedback may help you secure other opportunities in the future (although you should never be a slave to the feedback forms). There is much too much to be said about good teaching practice for us to address the matter comprehensively here. As with any activity, planning your time, thinking about the objectives (imparting knowledge and aiding learning) and reviewing and reflecting on your work will help you be the best teacher you can be. If you are engaged in tutorial or seminar style teaching which can involve classes of between three and 30 students then classroom management is also worth thinking about. Seek advice from more experienced colleagues and consider sitting in on some of their classes to see how they teach. While you will have certain ideas of how you should teach based on the best (and worst) teachers you experienced during your education you should also be open to new ideas and to new teaching styles and formats. The whole academic discipline (and publishing industry) addressing teaching practice has been in full bloom in recent years. You may benefit from reading the odd article or two but remember to take all advice with a pinch of salt.

The greatest benefit of teaching is not career advancement but rather the intrinsic enjoyment of discussing and debating ideas—whether they are newly-minted or as old as the hills. Whatever type of teaching experience you obtain make sure you take the opportunity to air any thoughts you have about your field. Students seek inspiration as much as they expect information and being taught by bright scholars who are conducting new and exciting research makes for a wonderful learning experience. Teaching clever pupils is also rewarding especially if you use the opportunity to discuss and debate your own ideas (remembering to cover any syllabus of course). Time spent in the classroom can also act as an antidote to the isolating experience of writing a doctoral thesis and energise you for other work.

Teaching experience will also allow you to test your commitment to a career in academia. As with all jobs there are parts of the post that will try your patience. Teaching the same tutorial for the fourth or fifth time in a row requires a willingness to engage with each class's own unique learning experience and to ignore the fact that you've explained *habeas corpus* several times already that day. Few if any university teachers enjoy the examination process which still involves a large amount of time sitting with a mug of coffee deciphering badly-written exam scripts and then arguing about the marks with a colleague. In addition the modern academic is required to carry much of the administrative load associated with teaching themselves. The days of secretaries and assistants are largely behind us and at times the paperwork required for each student can seem oppressive. If you find yourself struggling with some aspects of the job you are not alone—what you have to decide is whether the other benefits of an academic career compensate for the less savoury parts of the job.

If you are unable to secure teaching experience during the course of your degree but wish to pursue a career in academia explore other options that will help you tick that box on the recruitment checklist. Offer to act as teaching assistant on one of your supervisor's courses for a term. You may be able to give one or two lectures on your area of expertise and participate in the examination process. Some institutions now offer qualifications in university teaching and academic practice to their staff and students. If your university has such a programme be sure to enrol on it. Even if you don't need the qualification to secure a position it is likely that you will be expected to complete such a course during the early years of your career. If nothing else, the commitment to your chosen career path will be attractive to any potential recruitment panels you may face.

THE NEED TO NETWORK

The rather old adage that 'it's not what you know, it's who you know' still has a certain currency today. Although most academic positions are advertised with research or teaching needs uppermost in the job criteria there is still a great benefit in knowing the institutions to which you may be applying for positions and having your work recognised and appreciated even before your application lands on the recruiters' desk. It's not so much who you know as it is who knows you. If you're applying for a position in European labour law then it makes sense for your institution to ask its labour (or European) lawyers about your work before interview. If those who are consulted are aware of your work and think favourably of it then you may have an advantage before you even go into the interview. In the most extreme cases it may be that the institution actively tries to recruit you. However, even if you're not a prodigious talent being at least respected as a scholar in your field can stand you in good stead. To reach this point you need to publish—as we've discussed elsewhere—but also make good connections within your field and wider legal circles to ensure that you know what's happening.

Conferences, Seminars and Colloquiums

The most obvious networking opportunities are academic conferences, seminars and colloquiums. Attending academic conferences and seminars is a useful way to build your career. You should choose your conferences carefully—while there is often funding available, paying for registration and accommodation at a multi-day event can be costly when you're on a student budget. In addition, conferences take time away from producing your thesis, especially if you have to write a paper which isn't already part of your work. That point noted, if you have an eye on the jobs market you may find it useful to have one or two conference presentations or publications in an area beyond the subject of your doctorate—it will show that you have broader research interests and are not simply a one-trick pony. Whatever you present, going to one or two conferences a year can be incredibly beneficial, often in ways that you won't anticipate in advance.

Leo wasn't the most sociable of people and as such he had never really intended to attend conferences. In the middle of his second year, Leo's supervisor organised an event at his university and convinced him to present a paper. Leo hadn't realised how talking about his work with a new audience could prompt new ideas and help him to take his research in an entirely new direction. One line of questioning from an affable expert in the field prompted a significant rethink of Leo's theoretical approach. While other conferences he attended had a less profound impact on his work that one experience was enough to convert him to a conference-goer.

Different conferences can serve different purposes. A large general law conference will provide a wide range of networking opportunities but—unless the subject panels are very specific—will not necessarily provide you with the opportunity to obtain a detailed critique of your work. Good examples of these conferences are the annual events run by the Society of Legal Scholars and the Socio-Legal Studies Association. Your attendance at these conferences should be aimed at bringing your work to a larger audience than that which attends specialised events and making contacts in the wider academic discipline. Large conferences such as these are also well-attended by publishers and it can be beneficial to make contact with them with a view to publishing your thesis when it's complete. You may also benefit from engaging with the wider legal research discussed at larger conferences. There may be connections between your work and research in another field which you have not been aware of but which provide interesting food for thought. Smaller, more focussed conferences allow you to meet those scholars who work in your specific field and, if you present a paper, to discuss your work with prospective examiners, journal reviewers and future co-authors. These conferences may be more academically beneficial but they will be attended by far fewer people and so present fewer opportunities beyond the development of your research. You should try to attend at least one of each of these ideal-types (and some of all of the other types of events) during the course of your degree.

Attending the event is only half of the job though—to make it beneficial from a networking point of view you also need to participate. Ask questions in sessions. Remember that there's a difference between appearing (and being) interested and trying to prove that you're the cleverest person in the room. Asking a question and then following it up informally in the coffee break is a good way to start a conversation with a leading figure whom you've never met before. You should use whatever formal or informal meals and snack breaks there may be to introduce yourself to other participants. Approaching strangers and saying hello can be daunting but if you want to meet new people then you have to meet new people. If you are discussing an interesting journal article or book promise to email the title or citation after the conference. This is a good way of building on your initial conversation and continuing the contact after the event. Too often we just exchange business cards or email addresses and never look at them again. It's always pleasantly surprising to receive the follow-up email a few days later so be sure send one.

Even the most prolific conference attendee cannot be at events all of the time. For long periods between events you will need to research, teach and write. Nonetheless, there remain several means by which you can reach out to scholars and professional lawyers during such periods—whether by cold calling prospective contacts or participating in online discussion groups and internet communities.

Cold Call Email

'Cold calling'—contacting a person or institution without any prior contact—is a useful but difficult to use tool to make new connections. Writing a letter or email to a leading thinker in your field can open new doors for you and your research. The difficulty is in knowing who to contact and how to do so to ensure you get the best possible response (or indeed any response). Wherever your doctoral research project is based you may wish to contact staff at another institution to discuss your work or theirs or the relationship between the two. Often your research area will become so specialised that you will meet the few other experts at a conference or other event. In some cases your supervisor or another colleague may be able to provide you with an appropriate introduction—they may write on your behalf—but in other cases there will simply be no direct connection between you and the target of your intellectual courtship and so you will have to cold call.

Having identified such a person you will need to consider the appropriate means by which to contact them. In almost all cases today that will be by email. A hard copy letter has a certain advantage—it takes more time and so will be recognised as a thoughtful correspondence by the recipient. In the case of some scholars, particularly those with a more traditional mindset, this may be more likely to elicit a response. This same thoughtfulness may also be the downfall of a cold call letter. A thoughtful letter may need to be met with a thoughtful response and in mulling over how to reply, the recipient may forget the matter altogether. To avoid this it can be useful to include an email address or telephone number in the letter to make a quick informal reply easier.

Suggesting an email response to a written letter may simply be proof that email is more efficient and effective today—although it is not without its pitfalls. Imagine the volume of emails you receive on a daily basis as a doctoral research student. Now consider your position on the career ladder relative to that of your contact and the likely effect that has on the volume of email they receive. The difference may not be exponential but it's certainly quite large. As a result there is always a chance that your email may simply be lost in the deluge of genuine correspondence, departmental, institutional and network circulars and miscellaneous unsolicited nonsense that fills each academic's inbox on a daily basis. Your email needs to stand out and make it easy for the recipient to reply.

It's not easy to make your email stand out. You might consider including an interesting article or case which the recipient might find useful but might not otherwise come across. You could try marking it 'urgent' or using one of the other signifiers of importance built into email clients. However, this may simply serve to irritate or bemuse the recipient who will no doubt have their own ideas on what constitutes urgency. A more enticing method is to choose your subject line carefully. 'Enquiry from PhD student at Somewhereshire

126

University' is not as likely to draw the eye as quickly as a subject line that mentions the academic's work or your common research interest. While we all receive many emails every day there are relatively few that are genuinely interesting and a subject that invokes our research interests will be a welcome relief from more administrative topics. The text of the email needs to be *informative* and *short* but should also make clear to the reader *what you want*. If the email is a long rambling description of your research and why you think it's exciting and ends without any clear question or suggested action on the recipient's part then your chances of a useful reply are low. A good email might look like the following:

To: a.bigwig@elsewhere.ac.uk

From: a.doctoralstudent@somewhere.ac.uk

Subject: Arendt & Schmitt in post-9/11 Europe

Dear Professor Bigwig,

I am a second year PhD candidate at the University of Somewhereshire working under the supervision of Professor Otherwig. My thesis is entitled 'Arendt & Schmitt in post-9/11 Europe'.

I am aware of your work in this area and enjoyed your recent article on Schmittian analyses of US law.

Next month I will be in Elsewhereshire for two weeks between the 1st and the 14th. I would be very grateful if you had the time to discuss any overlaps in our research during my stay.

Yours sincerely,

A. Doctoralstudent

Why is this a good email? First, it introduces the student quickly and succinctly. Including the name of your supervisor might sometimes be risky—if they are a known authority in your area their name may gain you kudos but that's dependent on the recipient's opinion of their work. Second, the email makes clear that the student is aware of the recipient's work which is both a sign of good research and is also flattering. Third, and most important, it makes clear what the sender wants—a meeting to discuss common research interests. It is very easy for Professor Bigwig to respond to this email and thus a response is more likely to be forthcoming.

If you don't receive a response after a fortnight then you can consider following up with a subsequent email. You should mention that you had emailed already but try to avoid sounding impatient—the recipient owes you nothing. After two attempted cold call emails without response you might want to consider putting that particular contact on ice for the time being. Pestering someone who isn't replying to your emails is unlikely to make them more likely to reply.

Research Groups and Internet Communities

Online social networking tools were discussed in chapter four. Some research areas may have specific mailing lists run by research groups or other online communities for the circulation of news and other information. The leading scholarly societies will all have mailing lists for both their whole membership and particular subject specialities. Join the appropriate lists to keep abreast of what is happening in your field. If there is no online network in your particular area you could consider whether it would be useful to set one up and if so why not take a shot? Being the person who brings people together is a great way to raise your profile and to make useful contacts with those working in your area. For example, if your work crosses disciplinary boundaries you may find it helpful to set up a reading group in your university that is open to those from other departments. Not only will you meet people but you'll get a reputation as an effective organiser.

Molly was a doctoral research student who was good on email but not so good in person. After a particular conference she was contacted by a participant she had met at the conference lunch. Her correspondent, Huck, was much better at networking. Molly was heartened by Huck's emails and kept in touch. A year later Huck invited Molly to give a paper based on her research at an event at his home institution. Huck's networking resulted in a free trip to a stimulating conference for Molly and subsequently the publication of her chapter in an edited collection. Emboldened, Molly became more open and sociable at conferences and has since reaped the rewards. Random meetings have resulted in Molly publishing a brief student guide to her topic as well as co-authoring a paper with a leading authority in her field. The lesson learned: get in touch and stay in touch!

Meeting new contacts and staying in touch with your fellow scholars is an important part of academic practice. Remember though that you can spend too much time trying to stay in touch. Networking has been satirised as 'not-working' and it is easy to while away the hours through online 'not-working' (whether professional or social). As with any aspect of your studies you need to decide what you want to achieve and the time in which you will achieve it. And don't try too hard, this is an area where good luck is at least as important as hard work.

PRESENTING YOUR WORK AT A CONFERENCE

A good conference presentation is part art and part science. Too often presenters at academic conferences simply drone their way through an often lengthy Powerpoint presentation or printed paper without any reference to their audience. The result is a mostly bored audience that asks very few, if any, questions and a slightly chastened speaker. A good conference presentation is exciting and engages the audience from the start. It may even appear spontaneous and unprepared. Remember that Winston Churchill, famous for his witty put-downs, remarked that most of his off-the-cuff remarks were carefully prepared beforehand. The art of giving a good presentation is to hide the science of the painstaking preparation that may have gone into it.

Before you even begin to prepare your presentation you need to have your work accepted for presentation. In later stages of your career you may be invited to present your work at appropriate events. When you are starting out it is necessary to submit abstracts in response to a 'Call for Papers' from an appropriate conference. A call for papers is precisely that—an invitation for interested individuals to submit an application to present their work at the advertised conference. Most calls will ask you to submit an abstract in the first instance. An abstract is a short summary of the work you want to present that sets out the question to be examined and the manner in which it is addressed and gives a brief overview of the conclusions. Abstracts are generally between 250–500 words. When replying to a call for papers it is important to conform precisely to the specifications in the call. Do not include more words than asked for. Do not include citations if they are forbidden. Comply with any formatting rules provided. Doing so will show that you pay attention to detail and may endear you to the poor beleaguered conference convenor who is dealing with the many, many applicants who ignore these rules. Think carefully about what you propose to present—the abstract will be due several months before the conference and your work will progress in between abstract submission and the final presentation. Try to judge an appropriate selection of your work to present that will allow you to explore some interesting ideas while not being so ambitious that you are left too much out on a limb. While abstracts should be focussed you don't want to be too prescriptive. If you have not yet written your conference paper you have to allow for the possibility that it will evolve—focus on the big picture rather than the minute details.

If you are fortunate enough to be selected to make a presentation then you should carefully consider your approach. The first rule of a good presentation is that you must know your audience. The manner in which you present your ideas should be tailored to the knowledge level of your audience. At a large, more general conference you must accept that the average audience member will know less about the background to your research than might be the case at a more specialised event. If you are addressing a more general audience then you will need to make your work more accessible. Avoid jargon and unnecessary detail (while retaining necessary detail). In this kind of forum an interesting idea is much more likely to leave a lasting (positive) impression than a walk through the most recent few cases in your area. You may not be able to deal with every nuance of your thesis but you can give an overview of the deeper analysis while focussing the presentation on the key ideas you wish to impart. If there are experts in your field in the audience then hints of your deeper work may be picked up by them in questions afterwards. At a more specialised conference or seminar you can assume your audience knows more but it is still important to be able to adapt your presentation if it turns out you have over-estimated your listeners. If the presentation is to a small group you may be able to ask before beginning how familiar everyone is with your research area and use the response as guidance.

The second rule is to know what you want to achieve with the presentation—and be realistic. If the presentation seeks to impart too many ideas then you will either rush through the material or you will lose your audience. It takes time for ideas to sink in and so it is useful to introduce your idea, elaborate on it and then reiterate it in simple terms in concluding. On occasion conference presenters will try to say too little—but this is a rare occurrence and assuming there is indeed an interesting piece of research to be discussed the more brief presentation should lead to a longer and deeper discussion. What you seek to achieve will depend partly on the nature of your audience and partly on the nature of the presentation. Naturally, the longer you have to present your ideas then the more material you can expect to cover. However, if you are part of a panel then you need to consider where your presentation fits within that panel. If you are the first presenter you may be expected to introduce the ideas to be discussed whereas if you are further down the list of speakers you should engage with the ideas of those who spoke before you.

Having established what kind of audience you will be addressing and what you want to discuss you should decide how you are going to deliver your talk. Will you use audio-visual equipment? Will you offer handouts—which may vary from a printout of a Powerpoint presentation to excerpts of relevant legal authorities to a full paper? Powerpoint presentations can be quite useful if deployed well. Don't try to pack too many slides into the presentation and don't put too much information on each slide. Use graphics where you can but try to ensure that they are of sufficient quality that they will look good projected. If you do use handouts be sure to include your contact details so that participants can get in touch in the future if they wish. On some occasions you may be required to or may choose to distribute a full paper either before the session or during it. Handing out a full paper has the advantage of giving the audience an opportunity to read your thoughts later and allows you to speak to the more interesting parts of the work safe in the knowledge that more engaged members of the audience can read the work in full if they wish. While a conference paper is not expected to be as accomplished a work as a journal article you should nonetheless ensure that anything you distribute is of a sufficiently high standard to impress anyone who might read it.

On the day of the conference establish how the session will run in advance. Introduce yourself to the chair and the other presenters, confirm the order of speakers and the time limit and familiarise yourself with the mode of presentation—whether it is sitting at a table, standing at a podium or some other arrangement. During the session the chair will introduce you. You should focus on introducing the context of the research and the subject of the particular session. Always introduce your ideas, develop them and then conclude. Engage your audience in the manner that best suits your style—use humour if it works for you and respond to your audience. If they are bored you need to respond. Of course, you should not mix up concentration with boredom. If the audience cannot hear you they will soon lose interest. At the same time you should not shout—a booming speaker or one with an unmodulated voice will also cause the audience to switch off. While you can of course rely on notes, being familiar with your material will help you interact with your audience. At the end of the presentation you will usu- ally take questions. Pay attention to the questioner. You may wish to write down the question. It will give the appearance of interest (even if you're not interested) and if the questioner rambles you will be able to return to their points. Be polite with questioners, however impolite they may be with you. If a discussion becomes quite prolonged you may wish to suggest that you continue it over coffee—this will allow other questions to be asked. Finally, always thank your audience. They have listened to you and engaged with your work so be sure to express your gratitude. After the session is over you may want to linger briefly to allow more shy members of the audience to approach you for further questions. The lunch or coffee break immedi- ately after your session is when you will be most likely to be approached by others seeking further discussion. Use this time to establish new contacts and lay the ground for further discussions in future. If you were asked a particularly interesting question by a member of the audience seek them out, thank them for their thoughts and see if there is any further scope for discussion.

After the conference you should follow-up on any contacts made and consider what to do next with the paper. If it was part of your thesis then make detailed notes on any useful feedback you received. You may not want to revise the chapter or thesis section immediately but your notes will prevent you from forgetting useful points. Don't leave it too long to do the revisions though—no matter how profound the ideas that are sparked may seem they will be forgotten if left for too long. If the presentation was a success and you have a high quality draft of your paper you should consider publishing it. In some circumstances you will not want to publish immediately but in others publication can be beneficial. Talk the matter over with your supervisor to ensure you make the best decision for you and your thesis.

CONCLUSION

This chapter has addressed some of the wider career-building aspects of the doctoral researcher's life. There are no golden rules for career development and your success is as likely to be because of serendipity as strategy. The advice here that has worked for some researchers might not work for you. No matter how similar your career path may be to others', each academic career is unique—it's part of the fun! The key points to remember from this chapter are:

— Teaching experience is important and often rewarding but it is important that your research doesn't lose out. Balance your commitments to ensure that you become a rounded scholar.
— It is important to build a network of contacts in your area to help with your career development.
— Prepare your conference presentations well but be willing to throw your notes in the air and speak off the cuff if necessary.

This chapter concludes our examination of the process of getting a PhD in law. Three appendices follow. Appendix A provides a list of useful legal research resources and some websites that provide information on the university environment and jobs market in the UK. Appendix B provides a brief guide to bodies that fund doctoral research in law in the UK. Appendix C contains a list of some of our favourite 'blawgs'—blogs about law and legal research. For those who wish to read further the bibliography offers a list of books and articles that we have found useful in conducting our research, in supervising others and in providing informal advice to many doctoral researchers.

Appendix A

Useful Resources

There is a wide range of resources available to help with the research degree process. Here we highlight a few that may be of use. One of the best ways of staying on top of both recent developments in your field and new resources that may become available is to join one or two of the learned societies on law in your jurisdiction. We have listed some of the better-known ones, but there may be specialist groups in your field. Ask colleagues for advice on good networks to join.

UK UNIVERSITY ENVIRONMENT

Once you join a university as a research student you become a part of the UK university environment. As such you'll need to keep up to date with developments in research, the politics of higher education and the jobs market. These resources will help with your current awareness.

Vitae
www.vitae.ac.uk

Vitae describes itself as 'a national organisation championing the personal, professional and career development of doctoral researchers and research staff in higher education institutions and research institutes.' Its website has some useful guides on different parts of the research process.

Research Councils UK
www.rcuk.ac.uk

Research Councils UK is a 'strategic partnership' of the different research councils involved in funding university research. Their website is a good source of information about the current environment for researchers in the UK.

Higher Education Funding Councils

Higher education funding in the UK is controlled by funding councils. The largest of these is the Higher Education Funding Council for England (HEFCE: www.hefce.ac.uk). The Higher Education Funding Council for Wales (HEFCW: www.hefcw.ac.uk) and the Scottish Funding Council (SFC: www.sfc.ac.uk) carry out the same task for their jurisdictions. There is no funding council for Northern Ireland, where funding is the direct responsibility of the Department for Employment and Learning of the Northern Ireland Executive (www.delni.gov.uk/).

Higher Education Academy

www.heacademy.ac.uk

The Higher Education Academy is an independent organisation that is funded by all four of the UK higher education funding bodies. Its role is to promote a better student experience in all parts of higher education. The Academy conducts an annual Postgraduate Research Experience Survey which assesses the satisfaction of the UK's postgraduate researchers with their experience in their universities. Its reports can be found on its website.

Times Higher Education Supplement (THES)

www.timeshighereducation.co.uk

Originally a supplement to *The Times* newspaper and now a stand-alone magazine, this is a must-read before job interviews. It occasionally has interesting articles on the doctoral process. All articles can be read online for free. Law jobs are often advertised in the THES as well.

Jobs.ac.uk

www.jobs.ac.uk

This website is a one-stop-shop for academic jobs in the UK. You can search by discipline (for example, law) and by region. Most, if not all, academic vacancies will be posted here. There are also occasional posts for research studentships. If you have not already done so, you will almost certainly add this to your bookmarks by the time you graduate.

FindaPhD.com

www.findaphd.com

This website, which is in essence a commercial venture, is nonetheless used by many UK universities (and those further afield) to advertise their PhD programmes and studentships that may be available to fund studies. Its database is not limited to law but can be searched by discipline.

Guardian Law

www.guardian.co.uk/law

While *The Guardian's* law website is primarily the online home of the paper's reporting and commentary on law it also features stories on legal education from time to time. It is a useful resource for keeping on top of what's happening in the UK legal scene in general.

UK LEARNED SOCIETIES

There is a wide range of learned legal societies in the UK and so we have limited ourselves to listing those of general interest here. Ask your supervisor for advice on more specialist institutions.

Institute of Advanced Legal Studies (IALS)

www.sas.ials.ac.uk

The IALS was founded in 1947. Whilst attached to the University of London, the IALS serves as a national academic institution, its role being 'to promote, facilitate and disseminate the results of advanced study and research in the discipline of law, for the benefit of persons and institutions in the UK and abroad'. The IALS conducts numerous seminars and conferences and is host to a large law library with particularly extensive collections in foreign and international law.

Society of Legal Scholars (SLS)

www.legalscholars.ac.uk

Founded in 1908 and holding charitable status, the Society of Legal Scholars describes itself as 'the learned society for those who teach law in a university or similar institution or who are otherwise engaged in legal scholarship. As of Autumn 2010 the SLS had over 2600 members consisting of academic and practising lawyers in a wide variety of subject areas.' The Society has a reduced-rate membership for students and has about 15 different subject groupings. Each year the society holds a conference covering a multitude of subject areas, as well as a special section for students.

Socio-Legal Studies Association (SLSA)

www.slsa.ac.uk

The Socio-Legal Studies Association was developed in 1990 as some scholars felt 'there was a need for a more permanent organisational structure which would help to keep scholars in touch with each other, providing regular channels of communication and promoting and supporting the work of socio-legal academics.' Like the SLS, the SLSA holds an annual conference in the UK and has reduced membership fees for students.

Association of Law Teachers
www.lawteacher.ac.uk

The Association of Law Teachers is 'made up of law teachers from both higher and further education, and for over 40 years has played an active role at the heart of legal education.' Its website has some useful information about the teaching of law in the UK.

Committee of Heads of University Law Schools
www.chuls.ac.uk

The Committee is exactly what its title suggests—a body of the heads of each university law school in the UK that is funded by higher education funding councils. While it is not an institution you can join (unless you happen already to be head of a school), its website can provide some useful information on the university environment.

FOR FUN AND MORAL SUPPORT

Piled Higher and Deeper
www.phdcomics.com

This website, which publishes a new comic about three times a week, is administered by former Stanford University PhD student Jorge Cham. Cham's comics, though based on the US doctoral experience, travel well across the Atlantic and capture brilliantly the highs and lows of the PhD process. There's a top comics section which is a good place to start as a new reader.

PhinisheD Forums
www.phinished.org

The PhinisheD Forums describe themselves as 'the place on the web to find friendly advice and support as you struggle with your dissertation or thesis, and afterwards as you navigate the stormy seas of academia.' Based in the US, the forums provide useful support and guidance from others within academia who understand the PhD process and what it's like to go through it.

Appendix B

Funding Organisations in the UK

The availability of research funding at particular institutions and from research councils and other organisations varies widely from year to year. As a result it is impossible to provide an up-to-date list of funding available—even at the time of going to press. Instead, we list here the major funding bodies that provide support for doctoral research in law. See their websites for further information on what is available to you.

Arts & Humanities Research Council (AHRC)
www.ahrc.ac.uk

The AHRC is one of two research councils that may offer support for legal research projects. They describe their role as supporting 'world-class research that furthers our understanding of human culture and creativity.' The AHRC offers different schemes for funding and so you should check with their website and with your institution whether there is a funding competition to which you can apply.

Economic & Social Research Council (ESRC)
www.esrc.ac.uk

The ESRC describes itself as 'the UK's leading agency for research funding and training in economic and social sciences.' If your research involves empirical work or other socio-legal research then the ESRC may be more appropriate than the AHRC as a funding body. Again, check with your institution and the Council for guidance on funding available in any particular year.

Commonwealth Scholarships
www.cscuk.org.uk

Commonwealth Scholarships are available to citizens of Commonwealth countries (other than the UK) to study at universities in the UK. UK students have reciprocal schemes for non-UK Commonwealth universities.

The Commonwealth Scholarship Commission of the UK administers the scheme and can be contacted via its website for further details. Because of the differences in academic years between the northern and southern hemispheres, those thinking of applying for a Commonwealth need to begin the process well in advance of applying to a PhD programme. Competition is fierce.

Modern Law Review (*MLR*) Scholarships
www.modernlawreview.co.uk/scholarship.asp

The *Modern Law Review* is one of the leading general law journals in the common law world. The *Review* offers scholarships which are awarded in amounts between £5,000 and £10,000 (which may be renewed) for doctoral study in any area of law that is broadly within the publishing interests of the *MLR*. Applications take no set format, but you must include a statement of your research and have the support of your supervisor (or intended supervisor). The application will have to be submitted by the Head of your School—each School is limited to two applications per year.

Appendix C

Blawgs

The blawgosphere is a neologism used to refer to blogs that take as their subject law, legal practice and legal studies. There are countless blogs written on law and those gathered here are but the few which we frequently visit and read. We are always interested in hearing about new blawgs so if you know of any, do get in touch.

ECHR Blog
www.echrblog.blogspot.com

Run by Antoine Buyse of Utrecht University, this blog examines all things related to the European Court and European Convention on Human Rights. It features case commentaries as well as information on new publications relating to Convention matters.

EJIL Talk!
www.ejiltalk.org

EJIL Talk! is a blog affiliated to the *European Journal of International Law*. It is edited by three scholars based in Oxford, Nottingham and London. Its mission, it claims, is not to provide gossipmentary—but rather short incisive commentary into legal developments with an eye on the broader implications.

EU Law Blog
eulaw.typepad.com

The EU Law Blog describes itself as a 'web log about European Union law for students, academics, practitioners and anyone else who may be interested in it.' It offers a sometimes eclectic coverage of new developments in EU law.

Human Rights in Ireland (HrinI)
www.humanrights.ie

Human Rights in Ireland is the blogging outlet for a team of academic lawyers and provides current awareness and Irish perspectives on human rights debates. In addition to examining developments in Ireland, HRinI regularly features articles on UK, EU and international human rights law.

IPKat

www.ipkitten.blogspot.com

Despite the rather odd name (and equally odd URL), IPKat is a premier online resource for all that is happening in the field of intellectual property law. Blogs within the IPKat community feature a logo with a cat in a super-hero outfit. Strange, but informative nonetheless.

IntLawGrrls

www.intlawgrrls.blogspot.com

This blog provides a forum for 'voices on international law, policy, practice'. As is obvious from the title the voices are largely those of female international law scholars. A team of regular bloggers is complemented by a long list of guest contributors.

Opinio Juris

www.opiniojuris.org

Opinio Juris is a US-based blog that focuses on discussion of international law. It is well-regarded within the blawgosphere and in the wider academic community—as evidenced by the advertisements by academic publishers on the site.

SCOTUSblog

www.scotusblog.com

For those familiar with the acronym, the purpose of SCOTUSblog is obvious: it provides commentary on the contemporary activities of the Supreme Court of the US. Posts can be read by category and there are regular features such as the series of articles relating to the confirmation of Elena Kagan as an Associate Justice.

UK Human Rights Blog

www.ukhumanrightsblog.com

Run by One Crown Office Row chambers, the UK Human Rights Blog does exactly what its title suggests—it explores topical developments in human rights law in the UK. Regular contributions from the chambers' barristers are complemented by the occasional guest post.

UK Supreme Court Blog

www.ukscblog.com

This blog is a joint effort by Olswang and Matrix Chambers. It provides previews of forthcoming cases before the UK's highest court and analysis of recent judgments. It occasionally has interviews with leading jurists—most notably Baroness Hale in Winter 2010.

Short Bibliography

Banaker, R and Travers, M (eds), *Theory and Method in Socio-Legal Research (Onati International Series in Law & Society)* (Oxford, Hart Publishing, 2005)

Bartlett, K T, 'Feminist Legal Methods' (1990) 103 *Harvard Law Review* 829

Becker, H, *Writing for Social Scientists: How to Start and Finish Your Thesis, Book, or Article*, 2nd rev edn (Chicago, University of Chicago Press, 2008)

Coleman, J and Shapiro, S (eds), *The Oxford Handbook of Jurisprudence and Philosophy of Law* (Oxford, Oxford University Press, 2004)

Cowie, F (ed), *Stakeholders in the Law School* (Oxford, Hart Publishing, 2010)

Cownie, F and Cocks, R, *A Great and Noble Occupation!: The History of the Society of Legal Scholars* (Oxford, Hart Publishing, 2009)

Dunleavy, P, *Authoring a PhD: How to Plan, Draft, Write & Finish a Doctoral Thesis or Dissertation* (Basingstoke, Palgrave Macmillan, 2003)

Germano, W, *From Dissertation to Book* (Chicago, University of Chicago Press, 2005)

Harman, E et al (eds), *The Thesis and the Book* (Toronto, University of Toronto Press, 2003)

Cane, P and Kritzer, H (eds), *The Oxford Handbook of Empirical Legal Research* (Oxford, Oxford University Press, 2010)

Kumm, M, 'On the past and future of European constitutional scholarship' (2009) *International Journal of Constitutional Law* 401

McConville, M and Chui, W H (eds), *Research Methods for Law* (Edinburgh, Edinburgh University Press, 2007)

Murray, R, *How to Write a Thesis* (Maidenhead, Open University Press, 2006)

——, *How to Survive Your Viva: Defending a Thesis in an Oral Examination*, 2nd edn (Maidenhead Open University Press, 2009)

Park, C, *The Research Student Experience: Lessons from PRES* (The Higher Education Academy, 2009)

Partington, J, Brown, G and Gordon, G, *Handbook for External Examiners in Higher Education* (Sheffield, Committee of Vice Chancellors and Principals, 1993)

Phillips, E M and Pugh, D S, *How to get a PhD: A Handbook for Students and Their Supervisors*, 5th edn (Maidenhead, Open University Press, 2010)

Quality Assurance Agency for Higher Education, *The framework for higher education qualifications in England, Wales and Northern Ireland—January 2001* (Gloucester, 2001).

Rugg, G and Petre, M, *The Unwritten Rules of PhD Research* (Maidenhead, Open University Press, 2004)

Salter, M and Mason, J, *Writing Law Dissertations* (Harlow, Essex, Pearson Education Ltd, 2007)

Tiley, J, '50 Years: Tax, Law and Academia' [2006] *British Tax Review* 229

Short Bibliography

Vitae, *What Do Researchers Do?: First Destinations of Doctoral Graduates By Subject* (Vitae, 2009), available at www.vitae.ac.uk
——, *What Do Researchers Do?: Doctoral Graduate Destinations and Impact Three Years On* (Vitae, 2010), available at www.vitae.ac.uk
Wellington J et al, *Succeeding with Your Doctorate* (London, Sage, 2005)

Index

Academia.edu, 55
academic careers, 7–8, 120–3
academic community, 64–5
academic journals *see* journals
acronyms, 87–8
administrative law, 121
anthropology, 30, 35
applications, 23–5
articles *see* journals
Arts and Humanities Research
    Council, 26, 137
Association of Law Teachers, 136
Australian Research Council, 110, 111

bibliography:
    key authors, 43
    key journals, 110
    researching, 43
binding, 91
black letter analysis, 30–1, 32, 40
blawgs, 56, 139–40
Bloglines, 56
book reviews, 108
boredom, 75–6
Brown, G, 95
Buyse, Antoine, 139

career:
    academic careers, 7–8, 120–3
    choices, 1
    conference presentations, 128–31
    doctorates and, 6–9
    legal practice, 8–9
    networking and, 123–8
    post-doctoral, 120–32
case notes, 108–9
case studies, 5, 9, 14–16, 18, 20–3, 29, 35,
    36, 47, 48, 51, 55, 61–2, 74, 76, 77–8,
    81, 87, 95, 99, 100, 103, 108–9, 113,
    122, 124, 128
celebrities, 22
Central European University, 18
Cham, Jorge, 136

Chui, WH, 30
Churchill, Winston, 129
citations, 95, 110–11, 117, 129
codes of practice, 59–60, 66
cold-calling, 9, 126–7
colloquiums, 64, 107, 108, 124–5, 128–31
Committee of Heads of University Law
    Schools, 136
Commonwealth Scholarships, 137–8
company law, 7
comparative legal analysis, 37–8
conferences, 64, 107, 108, 124–5, 128–31
confidentiality, 50, 81
consultancies, 9
copy-editing, 119
Critical Legal Studies, 32–3
critical race theory, 33–4
current awareness tools, 55–6
Current Legal Research Topics database, 74
cyber communities, 128

data collection, 36
databases, 44, 53, 74, 134
depression, 80–1
Depression Alliance UK, 80
Derrida, Jacques, 102
diaries, 56, 67, 75
discrimination, 71
doctorates in law:
    admission criteria, 2–3
    career effects, 6–9
    codes of practice, 59–60, 66
    deciding on, 10
    European programmes, 18
    interruption, 81–2
    nature, 2–4
    other degrees and, 2–4
    statistics, 6
    transfer from MPhil to PhD
        registration, 63–4
    UK programmes, 16–17, 42, 63
    US programmes, 17–18
    value, 4–6

doctrinal analysis, 30–1, 32, 40
dress code, 98
Dunleavy, Patrick, 11
Durham University, 3
Dworkin, Ronald, 102

ECHR Blog, 139
Economic and Social Research Council, 49–50, 137
economics, 30, 32, 34, 35, 36
Edison, Thomas, 43
EJIL Talk!, 139
Electoral Commission, 8
emails, 126–7
empirical research, 4, 35–7, 53–4, 84–5
employment
　see also career
　part-time, 26, 27, 77
　unemployment, 6–7
　websites, 134
　work experience, 3
equipment, 53–4
ethics:
　ethics approval, 49, 50–1, 85
　high risk subjects, 51–2
　illegal behaviour, 51
　issues, 48–52
　principles, 49–50
　vulnerable people, 51–2
ethics committees, 49
ethnography, 35
EU Law Blog, 139
European Journal of International Law, 139
European University Institute, 18
examinations:
　appealing decisions, 104
　choosing examiners, 94–6
　dress code, 98
　examiner typology, 96–7
　format, 99–100
　internal and external examiners, 84, 95
　length, 94
　mock vivas, 98
　overview, 93–105
　place, 99
　post-viva corrections, 104–5
　practicalities, 99–100
　preliminary reports, 98–9
　preparing for, 97–8
　process, 94, 98–103
　questions, 100–3
　referrals, 105

significance, 99
supervisors' attendance, 100
UK v international practice, 93
verdicts, 103–4
video-conferencing, 99
writing and, 84
exercise, 81
exploitation, 70–1
ExpressO, 111

Facebook, 55
FeedDemon, 56
fees, 26, 77, 78, 81, 83–4
feminism, 33, 38
fieldwork, 36–7, 53–4
finance *see* funding
FindaPhD.com, 134
footnote surfing, 44
footnotes *see* citations
Foucault, Michel, 32
Friedrich Wilhelm University (Berlin), 2, 18
Fry, Stephen, 55
funding:
　arts and humanities, 26
　bodies, 26, 137–8
　options, 26–7
　part-time work, 26, 27, 77
　problems, 77–8
　scholarship applications, 25
　studentships, 26, 27

Gantt Chart, 56
gender studies, 35
Germano, William, 113, 117
Germany, 2, 18
Google Reader, 56
Gordon, G, 95
Greene, Graham, 79
grounded theory, 36
Guardian Law, 135

Hale, Baroness, 140
harassment, 71
Hart, HLA, 32
health problems, 79–81
HeinOnline, 53
Higher Education Academy, 134
Higher Education Funding Councils, 134
Holmes, Oliver Wendell, 32
human resources, 57
human rights, 32, 139, 140
Human Rights In Ireland, 139

Humboldt University (Berlin), 2
hypotheses, 42

illegal behaviour, 51
Index to Foreign Legal Periodicals, 53
Index to Legal Periodicals, 53
Institute of Advanced Legal Studies, 20,
    74, 135
institutions:
    choosing, 19–21
    league tables, 19–20
    reputation, 19–20
    research facilities, 20–1
integrated methodologies, 30
intellectual property, 140
international law, 139–40
internet communities, 128
internships, 8–9
interviews, 36, 42, 84–5
IntLawGrrls, 140
IPKat, 140
Ireland, 139

jargon, 88, 117, 129
Jobs.ac.uk, 134
journals:
    choosing, 109–11
    exclusive submission, 110
    law journals, 109
    notes for contributors, 110
    publishing outlets, 108, 109–13
    referees, 112
    revising submitted articles, 112–13
    status, 110–11
    submission process, 111–13
JSTOR, 53
jurisprudential perspectives, 31–4

Katholieke Universiteit (Leuven), 13
Kermode, Mark, 89–90
King's College London, 3
Kumm, Matthias, 7–8

land law, 7
language:
    good legal writing, 86–8
    Latin, 87
    second language, 18, 54
    skills, 38
Latin, 87
Law Commission, 8
law reform, 13, 31, 35
law reviews, 108

learned societies, 135–6
legal formalism, 32
legal practice, 8–9
legal realism, 32
legal schools:
    analytical, 30
    applied/integrated, 30
    black letter/doctrinal analysis, 30–1,
        32, 40
    choosing, 38–9, 40
    comparative legal analysis, 37–8
    Critical Legal Studies, 32–3
    critical race theory, 33–4
    discussion in thesis, 39
    early consideration, 30
    empirical methods, 4, 35–7, 53–4,
        84–5
    feminist legal theory, 33
    importance, 29–30
    internally-focused, 30, 31
    jurisprudential perspectives, 31–4
    law and economics, 34–5
    legal realism, 32
    postmodernism, 33, 34
    preliminary work, 39–40
    queer theory, 33, 34
    researching, 39
    socio-legal research, 34–5
    survey, 28–40
    types, 30–8
legislation notes, 108
LexisNexis, 53
LexOpus, 111
libraries, 18, 20, 53, 57, 76, 135
Liverpool University, 13
LLBs, 17
LLMs, 3, 4, 16
London University, 12, 135

Matrix chambers, 140
McConville, M, 30
mapping subjects, 43–5
Marshall, Barry James, 49
Marx, Karl, 32
Marxism, 33
media debates, 107
Modern Law Review Scholarships, 138
monitoring, 62–3
motivation, 4–5, 75–6, 78
MPhil, 63–4
MRes, 3
multi-disciplinary approaches, 30
Murray, Rowena, 11

networking, 55–6, 106, 123–8
NGOs, 9
Nietzsche, Friedrich, 115

observation, 36
Office of the Independent Adjudicator
    for Higher Education, 104
Olswang, 140
One Crown Office Row chambers, 140
Opinio Juris, 140
original theses:
    being novel, 45–6
    contribution to knowledge, 12, 43, 94
    development, 43–8
    discussing, 47–8
    exploratory writing, 46–7
    identification of central concept, 46
    identification of gaps in knowledge, 45
    mapping subject, 43–5
    rival projects, 73–5
Orwell, George, 86, 88

paragraphs, 88–9
parliamentary committees, 9, 64–5
parliamentary sovereignty, 87
Partington, J, 95
personalities, 65–6
Petre, M, 101–2
PhDs *see* doctorates in law
Phillips, EM, 45
PhinisheD Forums, 136
Piled Higher and Deeper, 136
politics, 1, 30, 35
postmodernism, 33, 34
Powerpoint, 99, 128, 130
preparation:
    applications, 23–5
    choice of academic subjects, 3–4
    choosing institutions, 19–21
    choosing supervisors, 19, 21–3
    choosing topics, 13–16
    funding, 25, 26–7
    overview, 10–27
    research methodologies, 39–40
    undergraduates, 3–4, 16
problems:
    boredom, 75–6
    finance *see* funding
    getting help, 81–2
    health, 79–81
    motivation, 75–6, 78
    overview, 73–82
    rival projects, 73–5

supervisors, 68–71
    writer's block, 78–9
proof-reading, 54, 90
publishing:
    academic journals, 108, 109–13
    necessity, 107
    overview, 106–19
    reasons for, 106–7
    self-publishing, 115
    student outlets, 109–13
    supervisors' help, 71
    theses *see* publishing theses
    types of publications, 107–9
    university regulations, 64
publishing theses:
    choice of publisher, 115
    conversion into monographs, 85, 86,
        113–19
    copy-editing, 119
    dissertation style, 117
    post-submission changes, 119
    referees, 116, 118
    revisions, 117–19
    submission process, 116
Pugh, DS, 45

Quality Assurance Agency for Higher
    Education, 12, 60
queer theory, 33, 34

racism, 33–4
Raz, Joseph, 10, 102
recording equipment, 54
referees, 112, 116, 118
references *see* citations
references (character references), 24–5
reflecting, 48
research:
    academic careers, 7–8, 120–3
    aids, 52–7
    assistants, 54–5, 77
    bibliography, 43
    development and supervisors, 60–2
    diaries, 56, 75
    ethical issues, 48–52
    facilities, 20–1
    groups, 128
    hypotheses, 42
    identification of knowledge gaps, 45
    mapping subject, 43–5
    outlines, 61
    preliminary research, 15–16
    process, 41–2

research ethics committees, 49
schools *see* legal schools
search strings, 44
teams, 42
undergraduates, 5
Research Councils UK, 133
Research Excellence Framework (REF), 20, 107
resting, 48
routine, 76
RSSReader, 56
Rugg, G, 101–2

SCONUL, 20
SCOTUSblog, 140
search engines, 116
search strings, 44
seminars *see* conferences
sexual relationships, 71
signposting, 115, 117
Skype, 99
social networking, 55–6
Social Science Research Network, 53
Society of Legal Scholars, 125, 135
socio-legal research, 34–5
Socio-Legal Studies Association, 125, 135–6
sociology, 35
software, 54
Spears, Britney, 55
STEM subjects, 26
stress, 50, 80, 90–1, 97, 98, 100
studentships, 26, 27
supervisors:
  academic celebrities, 22
  academic community and, 64–5
  academic exploitation, 70–1
  approaching, 15, 21–2
  attendance at vivas, 100
  choosing, 19, 21–3
  codes of practice, 59–60, 66
  development of research, 60–2
  discrimination, 71
  duty of care, 71
  feedback, 67, 70, 71
  flexibility, 61–2
  formal requirements, 59–60
  harassment, 71
  making the best of, 66–8
  meetings, 66–7, 70
  methodical approaches, 61
  networking and, 64–5, 126
  nominating examiners, 95

number, 59
organised approach, 61
overview, 58–72
pastoral responsibility, 63
personality, 65–6
poor supervision, 70
problems, 68–71
progress monitoring, 62–3
ratings, 68–9
sexual relationships, 71
students' responsibilities, 68
supervision diaries, 67
supervisory relationship, 58–66
thematic approach, 61
themes and bugbears, 21
surveys, 36
symposiums, 64, 107, 108, 124–5, 128–31

tax law, 7
teaching, 7–8, 120–3
theses:
  choosing topic, 13–16
  coherence, 11, 12, 86
  copies, 91
  discussing, 47–8
  dissertation style, 117
  identification of central concept, 46
  length, 41
  monographs compared, 113
  originality *see* original theses
  publishing *see* publishing theses
  requirements, 11–13, 94
  titles, 16, 116
Times Higher Education Supplement, 134
titles, 16, 116
topics:
  choosing, 13–16
  new developments, 16
  originality *see* original theses
  preliminary research, 15–16
  rival projects, 73–5
tuition fees *see* fees
Twitter, 55
typographical errors, 25, 90

UK Human Rights Blog, 140
UK Supreme Court Blog, 140
unemployment, 6–7
United States:
  blogs, 140
  Critical Legal Studies, 32
  critical race theory, 33
  doctorates, 7–8, 17–18

journals, 110
legal realism, 32
universities *see* institutions

vanity publishing, 115
victims, 51–2
Vitae, 5, 6, 8, 80, 133
vivas *see* examinations
vulnerable people, 51–2

Warren, John Robin, 49
Washington and Lee Law Review, 110–11
websites:
legal recruitment, 9
search engines, 116
social networking, 55–6
useful addresses, 133–8
Westlaw, 53
work *see* career; employment

writing:
audience, 84
drafts, 89–90
exploratory writing, 46–7
final drafts, 90–1
format, 85–6
from chapters to thesis, 85–6
good legal writing, 86–90
language, 86–8
overview, 83–92
process, 42, 46–7, 79
proof-reading, 54, 90
quantity, 89
revisions, 89–90
structure, 88–9
timing, 83–5
vocabulary, 87–8
writer's block, 78–9
writing-up fees, 84
writing-up status, 83–4

Lightning Source UK Ltd.
Milton Keynes UK
UKHW020636280820
368972UK00004B/128